Parenting
with a
Global Vision

RESPONDING AS A FAMILY
TO GOD'S INVITATION

Parenting with a Global Vision

Copyright © 2021 by Center for Mission Mobilization

All rights reserved. No part of this publication may be reproduced
in any form without written permission from the publisher.

ISBN: 978-1-947468-51-1

Published by Center for Mission Mobilization

PO Box 3556

Fayetteville, AR 72702

For more resources, visit mobilization.org/resources

Unless otherwise noted, all Scripture quotations taken from The Holy Bible, New
International Version® NIV® Copyright © 1973 1978 1984 2011 by Biblica, Inc.™ Used by
permission. All rights reserved worldwide. Scripture quotations marked NASB are taken
from the NEW AMERICAN STANDARD BIBLE®, Copyright © 1960, 1962, 1963, 1968,
1971, 1972, 1973, 1975, 1977, 1995 by The Lockman Foundation. Used by permission.

Translations

We desire to make this material available to as many as will use it around the world
in a way that honors everyone involved in the work. If you would like to translate or
adapt this resource to use in your cultural context, we are very open to collaborating
with you. There are guidelines for translators at mobilization.org/translation.

Printed in the United States of America

First Edition, First Imprint, 2021.

C: 08-03-20   M: 07-08-21 1:26

Praise for *Parenting with a Global Vision*

"*Parenting with a Global Vision* will inspire your family to have God's heart for reaching the world with the gospel. This guide is solidly grounded in God's Word, and it's so engaging! The activities and discussion questions will take parents and small groups from learning to living it out!"

—TOM CHILTON, DIRECTOR, AWANA EUROPE AND NORTH ASIA

"*Parenting with a Global Vision* is an amazing resource for families who want to respond to God's invitation to mission. In theologically astute and practically helpful ways, this new resource will give every parent the framework necessary to live out God's global purposes with their children."

—DR. BRIAN HAYNES, AUTHOR OF *SHIFT: WHAT IT TAKES TO FINALLY REACH FAMILIES TODAY*

"Families are central to God's mission. Discipleship of children into God's global purposes for His Church — by their parents — is paramount to the mobilizing of future generations. These lessons are clear and practical. Parents will be changed even as they are equipped. I love this study!"

—DENNY SPITTERS, PIONEERS, CO-AUTHOR OF *WHEN EVERYTHING IS MISSIONS*

"God has called you to launch your children into the world to make a difference for Christ. *Parenting With Global Vision* will encourage you in this mission. I pray that God uses this book to expand your vision for your family and equip you with an intentional game plan to shepherd your children in the grand calling He has for them."

—KIM BLACKABY, CO-AUTHOR OF *THE FAMILY GOD USES*

"*Parenting with a Global Vision* is an answer to prayer to help parents learn more about God's mission and how to engage in it with their children. It is a great resource to help parents understand God's call to families to be part of His story, align their parenting very intentionally with His mission, and raise the next generation to do the same.

—NOSA TUKURA, EXECUTIVE COORDINATOR, CHILDREN IN MISSIONS NETWORK

"*Parenting With A Global Vision* is a beautifully crafted resource that helps families find God's grand purpose together and navigate their way into the future, joyfully confident that God's promises will be fulfilled. I know of no better way to start your child's journey of participation in God's global plan than with Weave resources."
—DR. JAY MATENGA, DIRECTOR OF GLOBAL WITNESS DEPARTMENT, WORLD EVANGELICAL ALLIANCE

"*Parenting with a Global Vision* is a remarkable reminder that God wants to include each of our families as He finishes the final chapters of His story. This study will guide you towards the direction of fulfilling the Great Commission and the purpose of your life in building your family and a community that loves and follows God."
—PEARL GANTA, GLOBAL CATALYST, LAUSANNE CHILDREN AND EVANGELISM NETWORK

"*Parenting with a Global Vision* is yet another divine call to the body of Christ to pass the prime stewardship of children's ministry back to the parents. This tool is an ideal encouragement to guide parents from raising kids with good, but limited intentions to parenting in the limitless intentions of God."
—TARIKU G. KERSIMA, AFRICA DIRECTOR, HORN OF AFRICA MISSION

"Use this lively guide to help your family step into the great, global story of Christ bringing His life and blessing among all peoples. Filled with practical ways to lift vision, deepen prayers, and connect with God's work in the world."
—STEVE HAWTHORNE, LEAD EDITOR, PERSPECTIVES

"Latin America has many tools to awaken mission passion, but until now, I have not found one aimed at the family itself. This valuable resource addresses the need we have for parents to take up the responsibility to disciple our children and gives us a biblical, missional, and practical tool to do so."
—GERMÁN RICCA, DIRECTOR OF MOBILIZATION, COMIBAM INTERNATIONAL

Contents

Introduction

Overview

We're so blessed that you are holding this study in your hands. Great care has been taken in creating it for you! We hope it will encourage you as a parent, inspire you as a follower of Jesus, and empower your family to move forward together in new ways, in light of God's promise for all nations.

We've intentionally designed each lesson to provide time for you to reflect on God's promise and what that means for your own family. We've also created space for you to consider God's purposes through engaging conversations with other believers.

Personal Studies:

Each lesson begins with the Personal Study. The content is designed for independent learning at home. You do not need to attend a group session or watch a teaching video before beginning. Approach this study as you would a devotional book. Throughout the lessons, you will find:

- Scripture to help you learn and reflect on God's truth
- Activities and big-picture questions that help you process, integrate, and personalize lesson concepts
- Steps that help you apply learning to your own life and family

Group Discussion Guides:

At the end of each lesson is a Group Discussion Guide. This section is structured to help parents:

- Share reflections from their own personal study
- Process lesson concepts on a deeper level
- Apply lesson concepts within their own cultural context
- Work through potential barriers to application
- Encourage and pray for one another

How to Use This Study

Personal Study Guidelines:

Work through each lesson at home with your spouse, or by yourself, over the span of a week. Each lesson takes about 1-2 hours to complete. You can either study the lesson all in one sitting or over several days. Make sure to include the "Live It Out" section of the lesson. Give yourself time for reflection, allowing the Holy Spirit space to speak to your heart.

Group Discussion Guidelines:

After you complete each lesson on your own, come together as a group. Use the Group Discussion Guide at the end of each lesson to process lesson concepts, go deeper in applying them to your own situation, and encourage one another. Group times take about one hour. Optional ideas are included for groups that have more time.

Alternative Options:

If you wish to do this study on your own without a small group, work through the six personal study lessons at your own pace. You may use the group discussion section for additional reflection if you want to further your learning.

Some small groups may wish to read and discuss the personal study lessons together. In this case, parents are encouraged to complete the "Live It Out" section of each lesson at home following your group time. Be aware that some lessons will require more time or moments of personal reflection because activities were designed for parents to do on their own. If participants want additional reflection, they can work through the group discussion sections independently.

Sections of the *Big Story Series* are used in conjunction with this study. Download this companion resource for free from *weavefamily.org/bigstoryseries.*

Pre-Study Reflection

Prior to starting Lesson 1, set aside 10-15 minutes to read and complete the six statements below. In Lesson 6, you will refer back to your responses.

1. In my opinion, the best people to teach my children about spiritual things are
_____ because ...

_____

_____

_____

_____

_____

_____

2. I believe my children and I need to know what the Bible says so that ...

_____

_____

_____

_____

_____

_____

3. I think God blesses believers because ...

_____

_____

_____

_____

_____

_____

4. In my experience, more people don't follow Jesus because ...

_____

_____

_____

_____

_____

_____

5. I think the purpose of my family is ...

_____

_____

_____

_____

_____

_____

6. Jesus said, "The harvest is plentiful, but the workers are few. Ask the Lord of the harvest, therefore, to send out workers into his harvest field" (Luke 10:2).

When I picture the workers serving in God's harvest field, I see ...

_____

_____

_____

_____

_____

_____

Write out a prayer to God, asking Him to use this study to teach and equip you in your parenting journey.

LESSON 1

Stepping into God's Story

Only when we know the context of His

story can we understand our purpose

in life. God wants to include you as

He finishes the final chapters.

—THE TRAVELING TEAM

Our View of the Bible

Read this excerpt from an Indian fable:

Six men went to see an elephant, even though they were blind. The first blind man touched the elephant's flat, strong side and declared, "The elephant is like a wall." The second man touched the elephant's squirming trunk and declared, "The elephant is like a snake." The third man touched the elephant's sharp tusks and declared, "The elephant is like dangerous spears." The fourth man touched the elephant's tall, firm leg and declared, "The elephant is like a tree." The fifth man touched the elephant's flapping ear and declared, "The elephant is like a fan." The sixth man touched the elephant's tail and declared, "The elephant is like a rope."

[*How does this story illustrate the dangers of partial knowledge?*]

_____

_____

_____

_____

_____

The manner in which each man interacted with the elephant gave him a partial but incomplete picture of the animal as a whole. Many of us use a similar approach when we read the Bible. Which of the following actions describe your personal study of God's Word?

Check all that apply:

☐ READ MY FAVORITE PASSAGES OVER AND OVER

☐ STUDY GOD'S LAWS TO KNOW RIGHT FROM WRONG

☐ LOOK FOR ALL OF GOD'S PROMISES TO BLESS ME

☐ STUDY THE LIFE OF BIBLE CHARACTERS TO LEARN WHAT THEY MIGHT DO IN MY SITUATION

☐ SEARCH FOR WISE WORDS THAT HELP ME WITH A PERSONAL PROBLEM

☐ LOOK FOR VERSES TO ENCOURAGE ME

☐ SKIP PARTS THAT SEEM TOO HARD TO UNDERSTAND

☐ READ PASSAGES THAT HELP ME HAVE INFORMED DISCUSSIONS ON CURRENT EVENTS

☐ READ PASSAGES THAT DESCRIBE THE UNFOLDING OF FUTURE EVENTS

☐ STUDY PSALMS AND PROVERBS TO HELP ME

None of these actions are wrong, but by themselves, they lead to a fragmented view of God's Word that gives an incomplete picture of who God is, what He is doing in the world, and where we fit in.

A holistic view of the Bible includes these truths:

1 author

+ 1 main character

+ 1 unifying theme
_____

= 1 Big Story

Although many writers penned its content, the Bible has ONE AUTHOR who directed their thoughts by His Spirit. Although the Bible portrays the lives of many people, it has ONE MAIN CHARACTER—God himself. Although its events span thousands of years, the Bible has ONE UNIFYING THEME that connects them and moves history towards a defined end. Although the Bible contains 66 books, it is ONE COHESIVE STORY.

To envision how the different books fit together to create one cohesive story, we need to understand more about what the Bible's author has in mind. What do you observe about God's heart and intent in these verses?

Psalm 46:10 _____

_____

Habakkuk 2:14 _____

_____

Malachi 1:11 _____

_____

God desires to be known and worshiped around the world, in every culture. In fact, this will be the finale of His story.

God's Mission

Throughout His story, God is pursuing one overarching mission. His decisions and actions are rooted in this mission.

What is God's mission?

To be known and worshiped by people from every nation, tribe, and tongue.

Read Revelation 7:9.

[How does this future heavenly scene connect to God's mission?]

_____

_____

_____

_____

God's mission unifies the Bible's storyline and moves it forward. This mission is the backdrop for historical and current events. *Its fulfillment will usher in eternity.*

Think About It

Let's return to the elephant story. Imagine that after their limited encounter with the elephant, the six blind men returned home.

[*How do you think each man described the elephant to his children?*]

_____

_____

_____

_____

_____

[*As parents, why is it important to have an accurate and complete view of God's Word and mission?*]

_____

_____

_____

_____

We will miss the bigger picture if we interact with God's Word like the blind men did with the elephant ... and so will our children. It is within the context of God's BIG story and mission that our families can fully understand who God has created us to be and our purpose in life.

God's Strategy

God's overarching mission is incredible, but how will He carry it out? How will He become known and worshiped on a global scale, throughout many different eras? God begins by making an unbreakable covenant with one man and his family.

[In Genesis 12:1-3, what did God promise Abraham and his descendants?]

_____

_____

_____

[What would be the global effect of God blessing this family? (verse 3)]

_____

_____

_____

Blessing–God's grace and transforming power in the lives of believers; God-given resources (spiritual gifts, skills and talents, possessions, time, opportunities) to share the knowledge of God with others

Abraham believed God's promises by faith (Genesis 15:6). Some promised blessings were realized during his lifetime, but many would be fulfilled in future generations. God promised to bless Abraham's family for a purpose so that they, in turn, would bless the nations around them with the knowledge of the true God.

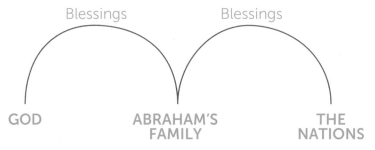

Blessings   Blessings

GOD   ABRAHAM'S FAMILY   THE NATIONS

Through an ongoing cycle of people receiving God's blessing and then passing it on to others, God would make His name great down through the ages.

This cycle continued from the Old Testament into the New Testament era when God's promise of blessing was fulfilled with the coming of His Son. Jesus, a descendant of Abraham, became the ultimate blessing to the nations. Through His death and resurrection, Jesus provided for all of mankind the only means of salvation and reconciliation with a holy God.

The cycle of receiving blessing and passing it on did not stop with Jesus' atonement for sin.

Read Luke 24:46-49.

[How did Jesus invite His disciples into the next
  phase of God's mission strategy?]

_____

_____

_____

_____

Empowered by the Holy Spirit, the disciples led the way in carrying the blessing of Jesus to the nations through the proclamation of the gospel message. Jesus' commission to "go into all the world" (Mark 16:15) was an extension of God's unbreakable promise to Abraham and his descendants in Genesis 12: "I will bless you ... and all peoples on earth will be blessed through you."

The Apostle Paul made this connection when he challenged believers to step into their part in God's mission.

Read Galatians 3:7-9; 29.

[How are believers connected to Abraham and the blessings
  God promised him?]

_____

_____

_____

Read 2 Corinthians 5:18-20.

[How do believers pass on this blessing to the nations?]

_____

_____

_____

Read Acts 4:12.

[*Why is it important that we bless the nations of our world today with the gospel message?*]

_____

_____

_____

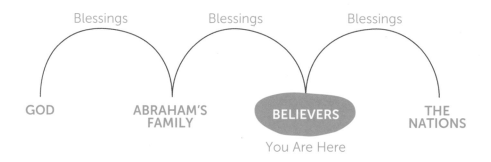

Blessings   Blessings   Blessings

GOD   ABRAHAM'S FAMILY   BELIEVERS   THE NATIONS

You Are Here

Here is where our present-day families enter into the cycle of blessing. As believers, we are recipients of the blessing of Abraham through Jesus. Through our faith in Jesus' saving work on the cross on our behalf, we become a part of God's family.

We receive this blessing—and we have a biblical responsibility to pass on this blessing of the knowledge of God to the nations. Every blessing of God—our spiritual gifts, talents and abilities, our possessions, our time and opportunities—are to be used to make Him known to others.

Cycle of Blessing

What does the cycle of blessing look like in the lives of people? Let's explore some familiar Bible stories to find out.

Read the verses in the God's Blessing column. On the lines below each person or group, record how God blessed them. Then draw a line to match each blessing with God's purpose. The first one is done for you.

	GOD'S BLESSING	**GOD'S PURPOSE**

(Daniel 6:16-27)   DANIEL ⦿

Sent angel to shut the lions' mouth so
that Daniel was protected from harm
_____

(1 Samuel 17:33, 37-50)   DAVID ⦿
_____
_____
_____

(Joshua 3:14-17; 4:19-24)   ISRAEL ⦿
_____
_____
_____

(John 4:7-26, 28-30, 39-42)   SAMARITAN WOMAN ⦿
_____
_____
_____

⦿ So the whole world would know there is a God in Israel

⦿ So that the peoples of the earth would know the hand of the Lord is powerful

⦿ So many Samaritans would know that Jesus really is the Savior of the world

⦿ So the peoples in all the earth would know that Daniel's God is the living God who endures forever

Look down through the blessing and purpose columns.

[*What do you notice about the blessings? What do you notice about the*
purposes? Summarize the pattern you observe of God blessing His people.]

_____

_____

_____

_____

_____

_____

In our day, God continues to use this pattern of blessing His people for a greater purpose that includes other people and nations.

Think About It

Add your surname/family name to the blessing cycle. Write it on the line in the diagram.

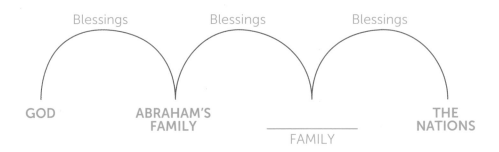

Blessings   Blessings   Blessings

GOD   ABRAHAM'S FAMILY   _____ FAMILY   THE NATIONS

What if your family believed that God wanted to use the blessings in your lives to reveal who He is and draw others to Himself?

[*How would this kind of vision affect how your family views the unbelievers in your lives? In your region? In the world?*]

_____

_____

_____

_____

[*How would this kind of vision affect how your family views the time, skills, and resources that God has entrusted to you?*]

_____

_____

Understanding that God blesses His people for the greater purpose of blessing the nations will help our family gain a balanced perspective on why God blesses us. Looking at the world with this blessing cycle in mind helps us recognize God-given opportunities and make choices about how we leverage our time, skills, and resources.

Live It Out

1. Memorize one verse that reflects God's overarching mission: Psalm 46:10, Habakkuk 2:14, or Malachi 1:11.

2. Find two pens with different colored ink, two color markers, or two colored pencils. Copy the verse below on a small piece of paper. Use one color for the blessing and a different color for the purpose. Place your verse card somewhere in your home where you will see it often.

God blesses us,
so that all the ends of the earth may fear [honor, revere] him.

(PSALM 67:7, NASB)

3. This week, read the story of Moses and Pharaoh from Exodus 7:1-5, 9:13-16, 12:37-38, and 14:10-18, 21-31. Look for the blessing and purpose revealed in this story. Pray that God will help you recognize His bigger purposes for the blessings in your life.

4. Download the *Big Story Series* for free from *weavefamily.org/bigstoryseries*. From One Big Story, do the "God's Power Demonstrated" family devotion found on page 11 with your children.

GROUP DISCUSSION GUIDE

Checking In (15 minutes)

Have someone in the group open in prayer. Before beginning the group discussion questions, briefly check in with one another about your initial reflections from the Lesson 1 personal study.

- What Bible verse or teaching point from Lesson 1 encouraged you or expanded your thinking?
- What activity from the Lesson 1 "Live It Out" section did you enjoy most?

Group Discussion (30 minutes)

Talk through each question, allowing all group members the opportunity to share their thoughts.

1. Even after witnessing Jesus' life and ministry firsthand, Peter still struggled to understand the bigger purposes in God's Word. Read Acts 11:4-18 and Galatians 2:11-14 together. What limited view of God's purposes did Peter (Cephas) hold? Think of a time in your life when you held a limited view of God's Word. What was the source of that view?

2. Before you completed Lesson 1, how would you have defined blessing? Review the definition of blessing on page 6. How does this change your view of God's blessing in the life of a believer? How does it change the way you see the purpose of those blessings?

3. Re-read the beginning quote on page 1. How does this make you feel? How does it change how you view your family?

OPTIONAL: Group Activity (10 minutes)

If your group has extra time or is meeting for longer than 60 minutes, complete this activity together. If not, move on to Group Prayer.

Have each person in the group finish these statements:
The thing I am most looking forward to in this study is _____.
My biggest insight from this first lesson is _____.

Group Prayer (10-15 minutes)

Close your time by praying for each other. Pray for God to:
- Reveal His purposes to you as you read the Scriptures.
- Reveal the blessings over which He has given your family stewardship.

LESSON 2

Discipling with Purpose

Your greatest contribution to the

kingdom of God may not be something

you do, but someone you raise.

—ANDY STANLEY

As parents, we want our children to come to know Jesus, to trust Him, and to walk in His ways. We desire that they become who God created them to be and live with a sense of purpose that impacts our world.

We need to consider not only *what* we want our children to become, but *who* is responsible for shaping their lives. Let's explore the major influencers in our children's lives during a typical week.

Influencers

One week has 168 hours. If we assume children sleep 56 hours (8 hours/night), then they have 112 waking hours. Use the knotted string below to think through who is influencing your children during these 112 hours.

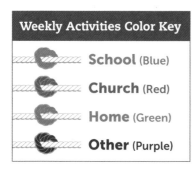

Weekly Activities Color Key
School (Blue)
Church (Red)
Home (Green)
Other (Purple)

1. Focus on one school-age child in your family.
2. Read the list of activities in the box.
3. Estimate, or keep a record of how many hours your child spends in each place during a typical week.
4. Using the Weekly Activities Color Key in the box, color the 112 knots on the string to show your answer.

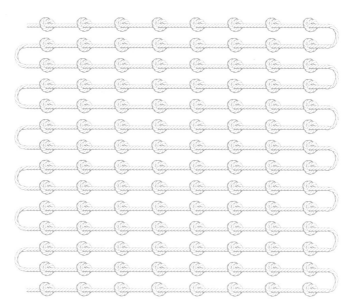

Now look at your colored knots to complete the ideas below.

My church leaders (red knots) have _____ hours per week to influence my children.

As a parent, I have _____ hours per week to influence my children at home (green knots). This is _____ hours more than my church leaders have.

Although the church plays an important supporting role, God chooses parents to be the primary spiritual influencers in their children's lives. Here is why.

1. Children spend more time at home than anywhere else.
2. Parents have the greatest access to their children and can observe their spiritual development on a daily basis.
3. Parents have ongoing opportunities to disciple their children throughout the week.

God chose parents to disciple their own children at home in the context of family. Write your children's names on the lines below.

I am responsible for discipling:

_____

_____

_____

_____

_____

_____

Family discipleship—parents intentionally investing in children's spiritual growth in the course of daily life by modeling their own faith and having ongoing conversations about God and His mission

Connecting Family Discipleship to God's Mission

[*In Lesson 1, we learned that God's mission is seen throughout all of Scripture. What is it?*]

_____

_____

We saw that God's mission strategy began with an incredible covenant, made to Abraham and his family.

The covenant God made with Abraham in Genesis 12:2-3 is shown below. Underline each phrase that begins with the word "I". Circle each phrase that begins with the word "you".

I will make you into a great nation, and

I will bless you;

I will make your name great, and

you will be a blessing.

I will bless those who bless you, and
whoever curses you I will curse;

and all peoples on earth
will be blessed through you.

The "I" statements describe everything that God promised to do. Look closely at the "you" statement.

[*What was Abraham's role in this covenant?*]

_____

_____

Although Abraham's role was small in comparison to God's, the brevity of Abraham's lifespan could hinder his ability to fulfill it. Abraham lived on earth for only 175 years (Genesis 25:7), but God's covenant extended thousands of years into the future.

How could one man, in one time period in history, fulfill his part of an eternal covenant? How could Abraham be a blessing to all peoples on earth?

Read Genesis 18:18-19.

[*As a parent, what must Abraham do in order for God's promise to be fulfilled?*]

_____

_____

_____

God's promise to bless all nations through Abraham was connected to Abraham's faithfulness in discipling his children and other members of his household. As a parent, Abraham was responsible for being the primary spiritual influencer of his family, teaching them to walk in God's ways.

At Abraham's death, he left a legacy that was in accordance with God's covenant. Abraham passed on a knowledge of the true God that would bless both his children and the peoples on the earth.

Read Genesis 26:1-4 and Genesis 28:10-14.

[*With whom else did God make the eternal covenant described in Genesis 12?*]

_____

_____

Abraham's God became Isaac's God ... and years later, Jacob's God. When Isaac and Jacob grew up and established their own homes, they were to direct their children in the ways of the Lord. God intended for their families to be spiritual influencers in the time and place in which they lived.

Read Psalm 78:1-7.

[How are generations a continuing part of God's mission strategy?]

Today, the God of Abraham, Isaac, and Jacob still carries out His mission strategy in the context of family, using Abraham's spiritual descendants (Galatians 3:29). Parents who know God and live out His mission disciple their children to know God and live out His mission. As family units, they bless the peoples of our world.

When children from these families grow up, they become the next generation of parents who cultivate the knowledge of God and His mission in their homes. These family units bless the peoples of their day ... and the process continues until God's mission is fulfilled.

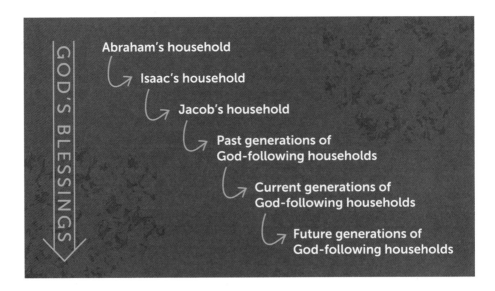

GOD'S BLESSINGS

Abraham's household
↳ Isaac's household
  ↳ Jacob's household
    ↳ Past generations of God-following households
      ↳ Current generations of God-following households
        ↳ Future generations of God-following households

Think About It

[How can discipling your sons and daughters to love God and bless the nations
cause your spiritual influence to extend beyond your lifetime on earth?]

_____

_____

_____

[How can discipling your sons and daughters to love God and bless the nations
advance God's mission to be known and worshiped in all the earth?]

_____

_____

_____

God's Vision for Family Discipleship

Here are common reasons why parents rely on the church to provide much of their
children's spiritual training.

Check 1-2 statements that you identify with most.

☐ LIFE IS BUSY. I DO NOT HAVE TIME FOR ONE MORE THING.

☐ I DO NOT HAVE ENOUGH BIBLE KNOWLEDGE TO BEGIN SHARING ABOUT GOD WITH MY CHILDREN.

☐ MY PARENTS DID NOT DISCIPLE ME AT HOME SO I HAVE NO MODELS TO FOLLOW.

☐ MY RELATIONSHIP WITH GOD IS NOT STRONG ENOUGH FOR ME TO SHOW MY CHILDREN HOW TO FOLLOW HIM.

☐ WHAT IF I DO THE WRONG THINGS? IT MIGHT CAUSE MY CHILDREN SPIRITUAL HARM.

☐ THE CHURCH HAS BETTER RESOURCES AND TRAINED STAFF TO DISCIPLE MY CHILDREN.

These statements reflect valid concerns about _when_ to fit family discipleship into our
home life, _what_ to teach our children about God, and _how_ to go about it.

There's good news. God understands our concerns and provides insight on how He
envisions family discipleship.

When?

Read Deuteronomy 6:4-9.

[*List moments during the day that God has created for parents to disciple their children.*]

_____

_____

_____

_____

God does not require parents to set aside two hours on Sunday afternoons to discuss the pastor's sermon or read long passages of Scripture. God does not expect children to sit for two hours and listen to a lecture on keeping God's commands.

God is much more practical. He invites us to engage with our children in conversations and experiences that deepen their understanding of God and His mission during the daily rhythms He has built into life. We will get to the how, but for now, let's consider when discipleship might take place in our families.

Think about daily family routines *in* your home.

[*List two times when you could engage your children in short conversations about God or His mission in your home.*]

_____

_____

_____

_____

Apart from church activities, think about weekly family routines *outside* of your home that involve both you and your children.

[List two times when you could engage your children in short conversations about God or His mission outside your home.]

_____

_____

Family discipleship is to be part of our daily routine, not isolated from it. Over time, even short conversations focused on God and His mission can build a foundation of faith in the lives of our children.

What?

Look at Deuteronomy 6:5-7.

[What are parents supposed to impress on their children?]

_____

_____

[What must be true of parents before they can disciple their children?]

_____

_____

A tea kettle can pour out only what is already inside it. As parents, we cannot pass on to our children what we do not possess.

We must understand something of God's character and His eternal purposes, and be growing in our own understanding of what a relationship with God looks like, *before* we can impress these ideas on our children.

We must seek to love God and honor Him in every part of our lives *before* we can show our children how to love and honor Him.

Children will learn far more about God and His mission from observing our actions than from listening to our words. A critical piece of family discipleship is parents modeling the heart attitudes and behaviors we want our children to embrace. Our knowledge of God must influence the way we live.

Doing what God commands in Deuteronomy 6 *does not require* a seminary level of knowledge or a background where we experienced family discipleship firsthand. However, it *does require* us to fill our minds and hearts with God's Word by reading the Bible consistently and to grow in our own faith.

Think About It

What is already in your "tea kettle" that you could pour into your children's lives?

Write your answers to the following inside the tea kettle:

- Two things I know about God
- Two ways I know that people can worship God
- Two things I have learned about God's mission

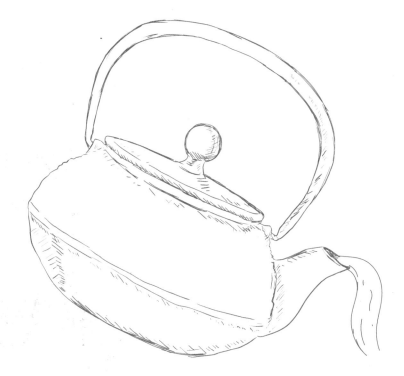

How?

In Deuteronomy 6:7, God instructs mothers and fathers to "impress" His commandments on their children's hearts. Impressing is a process that takes both time and repetition.

We have seen that parents are best positioned to disciple their children because they have many waking hours with them, access to their spiritual development, and ongoing opportunities during the week. However, these factors will not result in spiritual influence without the addition of one key ingredient.

time + access + opportunity + **INTENTIONALITY** = *spiritual influence*

Intentionality

Being intentional involves consistently using everyday moments and experiences during our week to build our children's understanding of God and His mission. What does intentional discipleship look like?

Intentional discipleship:

- Is ongoing, not a one-time event
- Occurs during normal family routines
- Is based on the truth of God's Word
- Connects children to God and His mission
- Is a two-sided conversation, not a lecture
- Involves short, daily interactions between a parent and a child or with the whole family
- Involves parents modeling what they are teaching in the words and actions of their own life
- Requires parents to purposefully seek opportunities and teachable moments

As parents, how can we use everyday moments or objects to connect our children to God and His mission?

In the chart below is an everyday moment that God has given us. Sunrises occur every morning, all around the world. Below the sunrise is an object found in most homes—shoes. Look at the truths about God that parents might share when their family watches a sunrise or while children put on their shoes.

Interactions are short, using simple words. References to Bible passages include phrases like, "God says, God promises, the Bible says" to help children know parents are not sharing their own opinion, but God's truth.

Now it's your turn to practice.

1. Find a common object in your home. Draw it in the box below the shoe.
2. In the middle box, write an idea about God's character that connects with your object.
3. In the last box, write an idea about God's mission that connects with your object.
4. Find 1-2 Bible verses that support your ideas and include the references.

Everyday Moment or Object	God's Character	God's Mission
	The sun rises every morning. We can depend on it. The Bible says God's love and mercy will never run out. They are new every morning, as sure as the sunrise. We can depend on it. (Lamentations 3:22-23)	God promises to make His name known to people all around the world. People will worship Him from the place where the sun is rising to the place where the sun will set tonight. (Malachi 1:11)
	God promises that He is always with us. There is no place your shoes can take you where God will not be. (Joshua 1:9)	God wants to use our family to take the good news about Jesus to those who have never heard about Him. God says we have beautiful feet whenever our shoes take us to tell others about Jesus. (Romans 10:15)

In His Word, God shares His vision for family discipleship. He lays out a plan that includes the *when*, *what*, and *how*. Parents, you are a big part of the *who*. God chose you to be the primary spiritual influencers in your children's lives, but He does not expect you to do this on your own.

God has given you what you need to intentionally disciple your children through His Word and by the power of His Spirit (2 Peter 1:3). Just as your children walk before they run, be encouraged as you take small steps to disciple the children in your family. For more ideas on using everyday moments and objects, see Appendix 11.

Live It Out

1. List fears or concerns you have about discipling your own children. Spend some time in prayer, giving these concerns to God.

_____

_____

_____

_____

_____

2. God understands our shortcomings as parents and promises to faithfully provide all the wisdom we need when we ask. Memorize James 1:5. Ask God to give you the needed wisdom and patience to disciple the children He has given you.

3. This week, use an object to teach your children something about Jesus. Afterwards, reflect on these questions: How did this experience compare to my ideas of what family discipleship would look like? If I did something similar with my children 3-4 times a week, what might be the result?

_____

_____

_____

4. Re-read Deuteronomy 6:4-9 on your own or with your spouse. Prayerfully ask God this question: "How do you want me to put this passage into practice in my family? What should I do first?"

GROUP DISCUSSION GUIDE

Checking In (15 minutes)

Have someone in the group open in prayer. Before beginning the group discussion questions, briefly check in with one another about your initial reflections from the Lesson 2 personal study.

- What Bible verse or teaching point from Lesson 2 encouraged you or expanded your thinking?
- What activity from the Lesson 2 "Live It Out" section did you enjoy most?

Group Discussion (30 minutes)

Talk through each question, allowing all group members the opportunity to share their thoughts.

1. In the process of creating pottery, designs and textures are added by pressing objects into the clay surface while it is still soft. This process is called "impressing." Why does God use the idea of impressing to describe the process of family discipleship? What does this look like in your daily life with your children?

2. Describe how an ongoing relationship with God was or was not modeled for you by your parents. What aspects of discipleship from your childhood would you like to incorporate in your own home? What would you like to add or adjust?

3. When you think about discipling your family in God's mission, does the "when," "what," or "how" come most naturally to you? Which presents the greatest challenge? As parents, how can you support each other as you seek to grow in the challenging areas of family discipleship?

OPTIONAL: Group Activity (10 minutes)

If your group has extra time or is meeting for longer than 60 minutes, complete this activity together. If not, move on to Group Prayer.

Have each person in the group finish this statement using one of the images below and explain their choice.

When I think about what I have taken in about family discipleship this week, it feels like _____ because...

Group Prayer (10-15 minutes)

Close your time by praying for each other. Pray for God to:

- Give you wisdom in modeling an ongoing relationship with God before your children, using both your words and actions.
- Give you a greater sensitivity to opportunities and teachable moments for connecting your children to God and His mission.

LESSON 3

Embracing the Nations

Personal Study

To belong to Jesus is to embrace

the nations with Him.

—WILLIAM CAREY

In Lesson 1, we learned that God's mission extends to all nations. He desires for them to know the truth of who He is and have the opportunity to worship Him.

We also explored God's strategy for carrying out His mission. God made an everlasting covenant with a family. Through Abraham and his descendants, all nations on earth will be blessed.

We saw how the theme of blessing the nations continued into the New Testament. Jesus commanded His followers to "go and make disciples of all nations" (Matthew 28:19).

In the context of God's mission, and His strategy for accomplishing it, we must consider what *nations* are in God's eyes.

Nations and People Groups

When we hear the word "nations," we usually think about countries—the nation of Japan, Kenya, Peru, or India. However, Jesus meant something much more comprehensive when He spoke about the nations.

Jesus used the Greek word "ethne," meaning ethnic groups. He was not referring to countries, but to groups of people who share a common cultural identity.

nations ≠ countries   nations = ethnic groups

In Lesson 1, we read about a future heavenly scene connected to God's mission. Read Revelation 7:9. Do you see the word "nation"? Both God's mission and its fulfillment focus on ethnic groups, not countries.

On the line below, write *ethnic group* in place of the word "nation."

> After this I looked, and there before me was a great multitude that no one could count, from every _____, tribe, people, and language, standing before the throne and before the Lamb. They were wearing white robes and were holding palm branches in their hands. (Revelation 7:9)

Revelation 7:9 shows us that God's mission is much greater than making Himself known to people in every country. Political boundaries are created by man, but God sees beyond country borders. God's mission is to make Himself known to people in every ethnic and language group, down to the smallest tribe or clan.

Each distinct ethnic cultural group in our world is called a *people group*. The thing that sets a people group apart—the thing that makes it unique—is its culture, not geographic boundaries on a map.

Consider India.

- India is one country.
- More than 2,700 distinct people groups live there.[1]
- Some of these groups have millions of people. Some have fewer than 100.
- These groups speak 1 of 22 official languages.[2]
- When members of these people groups move to another region or country, they take their distinct way of life with them. They hold on to much of it, even when surrounded by different people groups.
- God desires for all of the 2,700 people groups within India to know, love, and worship Him. Jesus commands us to share the gospel and make disciples within each people group.

> **People group**—ethnic group that shares the same language, history, traditions, beliefs, and daily way of life.

INDIA

Think About It

[*How does envisioning nations as distinct people groups rather than countries change how you think about God's mission and your family's part in it?*]

_____

_____

Same Strategy, Different Faces

In Lesson 1, we discovered a pattern where God blesses His people for a purpose that extends beyond themselves. Although specific blessings vary, the overarching purpose for these blessings is the same.

[*What is God's purpose for blessing His people?*]

_____

Down through the centuries, God has used the "blessed to be a blessing" strategy to accomplish His purpose of making Himself known among the nations (think people groups).

God's strategy is the same today, but the specific people groups who need to know Him have changed.

These ancient nations from Bible times no longer live on planet earth.

Here are some of the people groups who live in our modern-day world.

Who will God bless in order to reach each of them with the gospel message? Not Abraham, not ancient Israelites, not the 12 disciples, not Paul, not believers in the early church. They no longer live on planet earth … but your family does. Write your surname/family name in the empty circle.

You and your children are characters in the part of God's story that is unfolding today. It is no accident that your family was born into this specific time in world history. It is no mistake that you live in your current location.

In the Old Testament, Queen Esther's cousin reminded her that God placed her in a royal position in the Persian Empire … *"for such a time as this"* (Esther 4:14). God desired to use Esther to be a blessing in her day, and He placed her exactly where she needed to be.

In the same way, God desires to use your family, right from the place where you live, to be a blessing to the people groups who inhabit earth today.

On the lines below, write the current year and the country where your family lives.

My family is alive on earth in _____ (year).

We live in _____ (country),

for such a time as this in God's story.

Current Realities

If God's desire is to see people from every ethnic group worshiping Him, what is the status of His mission at this point? How close are we to seeing Revelation 7:9 realized?

In our day, the church has never been more culturally or geographically diverse, with hundreds of millions of believers. Yet, there are still about 7,000 people groups in the world who have yet to hear or learn about Jesus.[3] Their combined population equals more than 3 billion people.[4]

What does the spiritual situation of these 7,000 people groups look like in relation to the rest of the world? If we shrank the world population down to ten people, how many would know Jesus and how many wouldn't?

Spiritual State of the World

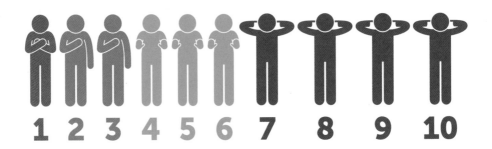

Out of 10 people in the world ...

| One knows Jesus as his Savior and Lord. | Two identify more with Christianity than with any other religion due to cultural or family background, but they do not have a relationship with Jesus. | Three have rejected the gospel message after hearing it. | Four have never heard the gospel message. |

Where do the 7,000 people groups fit in? They make up the last category in the diagram. Draw a box around the "people who have never heard" group (red).

More than 2,000 years ago, Jesus came to earth to bring God's ultimate blessing to the nations (think people groups!). His death and resurrection release mankind from slavery to sin and offer the opportunity for an eternal relationship with God.

Yet in the part of God's story in which our families live, 40 percent of the world's population has no way of accessing this blessing.[5] How is this possible? Let's find out.

Reached versus Unreached

Think about your own family. God has blessed you with different ways to learn about Him.

Read the list below.

Check everything that your family has access to in your home or community.
Underline everything that you currently use to grow and strengthen your family's faith.

☐ BIBLE	☐ CHRISTIAN BOOKS	☐ SMALL GROUP BIBLE STUDY
☐ LOCAL CHURCH	☐ CHRISTIAN TV PROGRAMS	☐ CHRISTIAN CONFERENCES
☐ BELIEVERS	☐ CHRISTIAN WORSHIP SONGS	☐ CHILDREN'S BIBLE STORY BOOK
☐ CHRISTIAN MOVIES	☐ CHRISTIAN RADIO PROGRAMS	☐ CHRISTIAN ONLINE PROGRAMS

Many believers have access to more items on this list than they actually use. Some have access to a few items listed here, but they make use of all that are available.

If unbelievers around the world completed this same activity, what might their checklists look like? Possible responses are shown below.

Unbelievers: Group 1 FULL ACCESS	**Unbelievers: Group 2** LIMITED ACCESS	**Unbelievers: Group 3** NO ACCESS
☑ BIBLE	☑ BIBLE	☐ BIBLE
☑ CHRISTIAN BOOKS	☑ CHRISTIAN BOOKS	☐ CHRISTIAN BOOKS
☑ SMALL GROUP BIBLE STUDY	☑ SMALL GROUP BIBLE STUDY	☐ SMALL GROUP BIBLE STUDY
☑ LOCAL CHURCH	☑ LOCAL CHURCH	☐ LOCAL CHURCH
☑ CHRISTIAN TV PROGRAMS	☐ CHRISTIAN TV PROGRAMS	☐ CHRISTIAN TV PROGRAMS
☑ CHRISTIAN CONFERENCES	☐ CHRISTIAN CONFERENCES	☐ CHRISTIAN CONFERENCES
☑ BELIEVERS	☑ BELIEVERS	☐ BELIEVERS
☑ CHRISTIAN WORSHIP SONGS	☑ CHRISTIAN WORSHIP SONGS	☐ CHRISTIAN WORSHIP SONGS
☑ CHILDREN'S BIBLE STORY BOOK	☐ CHILDREN'S BIBLE STORY BOOK	☐ CHILDREN'S BIBLE STORY BOOK
☑ CHRISTIAN MOVIES	☐ CHRISTIAN MOVIES	☐ CHRISTIAN MOVIES
☑ CHRISTIAN RADIO PROGRAMS	☑ CHRISTIAN RADIO PROGRAMS	☐ CHRISTIAN RADIO PROGRAMS
☑ CHRISTIAN ONLINE PROGRAMS	☑ CHRISTIAN ONLINE PROGRAMS	☐ CHRISTIAN ONLINE PROGRAMS

Look carefully at how unbelievers completed this activity.

[*What do you observe about the unbelievers in Group 1 and 2? How does this differ from the unbelievers in Group 3?*]

_____

_____

_____

_____

Some unbelievers (like Groups 1 and 2) live in people groups that have access to materials, programs, and people that can help them learn about God. They can get a Bible or Christian books in their language, attend a local Christian church, make use of Christian media, or talk to believers in their community ... but they choose not to.

These unbelievers belong to a **REACHED** people group.

Some unbelievers (Group 3 example) live in people groups that do not have access to *any* materials, programs, or people that can help them learn about God—no Bibles or Christian books in their language, no Christian churches, no Christian media, and no believers in their entire region who reflect Jesus. Linguistic, cultural, or geographic barriers block these unbelievers' access to the gospel. This is their reality ... not their choice.

These unbelievers belong to an **UNREACHED** people group.

The major difference between reached and unreached peoples is not their spiritual state, but their *access* to the gospel.

Look back at the Spiritual State of the World diagram on page 36. The 40 percent of the world who has yet to hear or learn about Jesus, due to lack of access to believers or resources, are part of 7,000 *unreached* people groups. Above the box you drew, write the word "unreached."

Our world is home to billions of unreached peoples who are born, live, and die without ever meeting a single follower of Jesus or hearing the good news of the eternal hope He offers them.

Our world is also home to millions of Jesus-following families like yours who live in proximity to unreached peoples or have the potential to take the gospel to them ... but first, Jesus-following families must understand and embrace God's mission and purpose for blessing them.

Think About It

[*Compare unbelievers in reached and unreached cultures. How are they the same? How are they different?*]

_____

_____

[*If you looked at your family's life through a "for such a time as this" lens, how might it change your priorities?*]

_____

_____

Belief Systems

Your family has a belief system that influences your thoughts, attitudes, and behaviors ... so do families in unreached people groups.

As parents, you desire for your children to embrace what you teach them about God. You want them to grow into lifelong followers of Jesus. Families in unreached people groups pass on their religious beliefs and practices in much the same way that you do ... from parents to children in the home, with the support of religious and educational institutions in their community.

But there is a major difference between your family and theirs! The beliefs and practices of unreached peoples are not based on the truth of God's Word. Unless the gospel of Jesus enters into an unreached people group, the same false beliefs and practices will continue in the next generation.

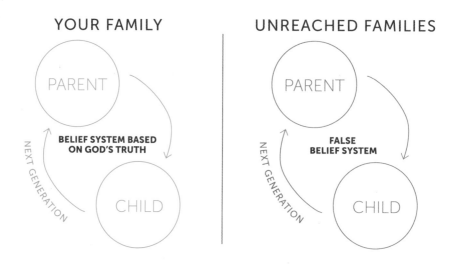

If unreached families have never heard about Jesus, what do they believe? The majority belong to one of these five major religious blocs:

ANIMIST   HINDU   ATHEIST   MUSLIM   BUDDHIST

Some unreached families incorporate practices from several belief systems in their daily lives. For detailed information on beliefs and practices of each religious bloc, see the Additional Resources section.

Read John 14:6.

[Why is it important to break the belief systems of families in these religious blocs?]

_____

_____

_____

Few believers are working among unreached people groups who embrace false belief systems. Less than 10 percent of cross-cultural workers serve among unreached people groups.[6] Of all money given to support mission efforts, only two percent is used for ministry among those who have no access to the good news of Jesus.[7]

Hope in God

At this point, you may feel overwhelmed and discouraged by the spiritual situation of billions of the world's peoples. As believers, we want to align our hearts with God's and pursue what matters most to Him ... but what can one family do when the spiritual needs are so great?

Be encouraged! You are not acting on your own. The all-powerful God of the universe invites your family to partner with Him in what He is already bringing about.

Read Isaiah 46:9-11.

[How does this passage encourage you?]

_____

_____

God will accomplish His eternal purposes. Some day, believers from every people group will worship together before His throne, just as Revelation 7:9 declares. They will experience the joy of an eternal relationship with their Creator, and God will receive the glory He deserves.

This future reality allows our families to serve from a place of promise and hope as we join God in bringing the good news of Jesus to the unreached peoples of our day.

Think About It

Reflect on what you have learned about God's mission, His strategy for accomplishing it, and the current spiritual state of the world.

[*Why is it important for your family to learn about unreached peoples?*]

_____

_____

_____

_____

_____

[*As a parent, what is one step you can take to begin learning about unreached peoples yourself?*]

_____

_____

_____

_____

_____

[*What is one way you could begin to introduce the concepts from this lesson to your family?*]

_____

_____

_____

_____

_____

Live It Out

1. This week, read and meditate on these hopeful verses about the nations (people groups): Psalm 22:27, Psalm 86:9, Matthew 12:21, and Revelation 15:4.

2. Read the people group profile below on the Rajput people. With your spouse or by yourself, pray for them for five minutes each day for a week.

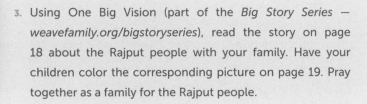

3. Using One Big Vision (part of the *Big Story Series — weavefamily.org/bigstoryseries*), read the story on page 18 about the Rajput people with your family. Have your children color the corresponding picture on page 19. Pray together as a family for the Rajput people.

4. Hang a world map in your home. Locate where the Rajput people live. Continue to use the map to locate where unreached peoples live as you learn about and pray for them. Download a free world map from *weavefamily.org/map*.

People Group Profile:

People Group: Rajput

Location: India

Population: 45-46 million

Religion: Hinduism

Christian: 0.02% percent

Evangelical Christian: unknown

Historically, the Rajput were warriors who defended the kings of India. As a part of the nobility, they enjoyed a high position in society. Today, many are respected landowners. Men farm while women look after the livestock and care for their children. Rajput men wear turbans which are tied to represent their specific clan. Most Rajputs are Hindus who believe in millions of different gods and goddesses. They primarily worship Shiva (the destroyer), Surya (the sun god), and Durga (the mother of the universe). The number of Rajputs who believe in Jesus is so small that they cannot be accurately counted.

GROUP DISCUSSION GUIDE

Checking In (15 minutes)

Have someone in the group open in prayer. Before beginning the group discussion questions, briefly check in with one another about your initial reflections from the Lesson 3 personal study.

- What Bible verse or teaching point from Lesson 3 encouraged you or expanded your thinking?
- What activity from the Lesson 3 "Live It Out" section did you enjoy most?

Group Discussion (30 minutes)

Talk through each question, allowing all group members the opportunity to share their thoughts.

1. Briefly share about people who planted seeds about Jesus in your life or led you to faith in Christ. Imagine that you were part of an unreached people group and there were no believers in your entire region who could tell you about Jesus. How might your life have been different? Read Psalm 67:1-2 together. What responsibility do we have to the unreached peoples of our world today?

2. Do you know someone who embraces animism, Hinduism, atheism, Islam, or Buddhism? Share how you met and any steps you have taken to develop a relationship with them. Include insights into their beliefs that you have gained or specific opportunities God has presented for you to share your faith with them.

3. If you are not currently aware of any unreached people groups near you, how might your family find out which groups live in your city or country? Think through who you might ask and what resources you have access to that could help you learn more.

OPTIONAL: Group Activity (10 minutes)

If your group has extra time or is meeting for longer than 60 minutes, complete this activity together. If not, move on to Group Prayer.

Read the statement below. Have each person check the idea that most reflects his/her response to the current reality of unreached peoples and explain their choice.

When I learned that more than 3 billion people have never heard the good news of Jesus, I felt _____ because...

☐ DEEP SADNESS	☐ GUILT/SHAME	☐ EXCITED BY THE OPPORTUNITY TO RESPOND
☐ SURPRISE/SHOCK	☐ COMPASSION	
☐ DEEPLY BURDENED	☐ A SENSE OF DESPAIR	

Group Prayer (10-15 minutes)

Close your time by praying for each other. Pray for God to:
- Give you His compassion towards unreached people groups.
- Connect you to opportunities for your family to learn about and build relationships with people from unreached groups.

LESSON 4

Joining in God's Mission

God involves us in His mission not because
He needs us, but because He loves us. And
in His mercy He has invited us to be involved
in His sovereign design for the spread of
the gospel to the ends of the earth.

—DAVID PLATT

Invitation

Think back to a time when you received an invitation. A relative, friend, or co-worker asked you to join in celebrating a special occasion. Your participation was not required, but rather highly desired. The host did not need your help to pull off the event, nor would it be canceled if you did not attend. Because of your relationship, the host invited you to join in what he had already set in motion so that you could experience the joy of that day.

God is issuing an invitation to families just like yours. If you love and follow Jesus, God invites you to join Him in His mission. He is already doing a tremendous work in our day and He desires for your family to participate alongside Him. God wants you and your children to experience the joy of seeing the unreached peoples of our world come into a relationship with Him.

God's Work

God is inviting our families into His work, a work that began before the foundation of the world. Let's look more closely at God's work to find out where we fit into His plans.

Read Romans 5:6-8, 6:22-23.

[*What part of God's work has He already completed?*]

_____

_____

_____

Read Luke 19:10 and Matthew 28:18-20.

[*What work is God still doing in our day?*]

_____

_____

_____

Read John 20:21 and Acts 1:8.

[*Who invites and empowers our families to join in God's work?*]

_____

_____

_____

Read Revelation 7:9.

[*What will it look like when God's work is completed?*]

_____

_____

_____

In the invitation below, add your family name/surname.

GOD INVITES

THE _____ FAMILY

TO JOIN WITH HIM IN HIS WORK

OF BLESSING UNREACHED PEOPLE GROUPS

WITH THE GOOD NEWS OF JESUS.

World Christian Habits

As our families come to understand God's love for the world, our desire to see Him glori-fied among all people groups will grow. God's mission becomes central to who we are as believers and influences our thoughts, conversations, and actions. We begin to live in an intentional way to make God known among the nations. We become *World Christians*.

As World Christian families, we can join in God's work and become a blessing to unreached people groups in various ways. The five practices we will explore in this lesson are:

Pray   Welcome   Go   Send   Mobilize

These practices are called *World Christian habits*.

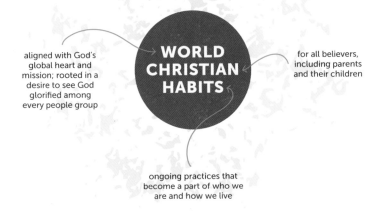

aligned with God's global heart and mission; rooted in a desire to see God glorified among every people group

WORLD CHRISTIAN HABITS

for all believers, including parents and their children

ongoing practices that become a part of who we are and how we live

In the diagram above, look carefully at the breakdown of each word in the circle. Use this information to answer the three questions below.

[*What is the motivation behind living out these habits?*]

_____

[*Who can participate in these habits?*]

_____

[*How do these habits impact our lives?*]   ☐ one-time action   ☐ ongoing actions

Habit: Pray

Our prayers include different elements like adoration, thanksgiving, and confession. One strategic way for your family to bless unreached people groups is through ongoing intercessory prayer.

Read Luke 10:2 and 1 Timothy 2:1, 3-4.

[What do these verses urge believers to do and why?]

_____

_____

[What does obedience to these verses look like in the life of a family?]

_____

_____

Perhaps you already pray with your family each day—before a meal, before or after school, at bedtime, or when a specific issue arises. Intercession for the unreached can be an extension of prayer times which are already part of your regular routine.

[List 1-2 times during the day when you could engage your family in prayer for the unreached.]

_____

_____

You may already pray for unbelieving relatives, co-workers, and friends to come to know Jesus as Savior. Knowing people personally makes it easier to pray in specific ways.

Interceding for unreached peoples that you have never met seems more difficult. Even though you may not know their names, the One who hears and answers your prayers *does*.

> **Praying**—ongoing practice of interceding for the spiritual needs of unreached peoples; asking God to send laborers to those with no access to the gospel

You may not be aware of specific concerns that unreached families have, but you do know their greatest need—to come to know Jesus.

As you begin to incorporate the practice of praying for the unreached in your home, let God's Word guide you.

Look at the chart below. The first column lists verses which reflect God's promises for the nations (people groups), something God has done to provide our salvation, or our spiritual state without Jesus. In the second column, the verse is used to form a simple intercessory prayer.

God's Word	My Prayers
All the nations you have made will come and worship before you, Lord; they will bring glory to your name. (Psalm 86:9)	God, You created every nation for Your glory. I pray that families in unreached people groups will have the opportunity to come to know and worship You.
Jesus answered, "I am the way and the truth and the life. No one comes to the Father except through me." (John 14:6)	God, I pray that the unreached peoples will come to know Jesus, the only way to come into a relationship with You.

Now it's your turn to practice.

1. Grab your Bible and read John 3:16-17, Romans 1:16, and Colossians 1:13-14.
2. Choose one passage and write the verse and reference in the God's Word column.
3. Turn your verse into a prayer for the unreached. Write it in the My Prayers column.

For more verses, see Appendix I. There are many ways to intercede for the unreached, so get creative, try different ideas, and discover what works best for your family.

Praying for unreached peoples changes their current reality. When we pray in accordance with God's desire for the unreached, we can be confident that He hears us. God removes barriers that prevent people groups from having access to the gospel, softens hearts to receive the good news of Jesus, opens minds that are blinded by false belief systems, and calls out more workers into His harvest field.

Praying for unreached peoples also changes our families. As we pray, God begins to cultivate in us hearts of compassion for the peoples that He loves, especially for those without access to the gospel. Instead of viewing them as a faceless crowd or a sad statistic, we start to view the unreached through God's eyes as:

- peoples of value that God created, loves, and wants to redeem
- peoples who are like lost sheep without a shepherd
- peoples from whom God is worthy to receive worship

Habit: Welcome

Our families live in a world on the move. Millions of people relocate to other regions and countries each year. Many settle permanently. Whether by choice or circumstances beyond their control, every person moves for a specific reason. God uses, and even initiates, these moves for His own purposes ... purposes that are in line with His mission.

Read Leviticus 19:33-34 and Acts 17:26-27 to find out what God desires for people who relocate. Then complete the second section of the chart below.

Why People Move	How God Uses Moves
Seek education, jobs, ways to provide for their family, freedom, safety, or a better future.	
Escape violence, harsh physical environments, restrictive governments, persecution, or discrimination.	

Many on-the-move people come from areas with little or no access to the gospel. They often settle in areas where they will have multiple opportunities to hear about Jesus and interact with believers.

This is where your family comes in. God is bringing unreached peoples right to your doorstep and giving you the opportunity to bless them through the habit of *welcoming*. The first step is intentionally seeking out people from other cultures who live, study, or work in your community.

Depending on your family's location, they might include: international scholars, shop owners, restaurant workers, taxi drivers, business professionals, factory workers, househelpers, or refugee families.

> **Welcoming**—ongoing practice of initiating and building friendships with people from other cultures who live in our community; includes hospitality, meeting needs, and looking for opportunities to share about Jesus

[*In your community, where do you see people from other cultures? From what regions or countries do they come?*]

_____

_____

_____

_____

_____

Most of these people are eager to learn about your culture, including your family's beliefs about God. Many will need help to navigate unfamiliar systems, and families like yours can assist them in practical ways. For example, a group of believers in Brazil helped newly-arrived Syrian refugees to register their children for school. Other ways to engage with foreigners include helping them use public transportation or learn the national language.

You can also invite them to join you for coffee/tea, or arrange a time for your children to play with theirs. All foreigners are longing for connection and friendship in a sea of strangers. Through welcoming, *your family can become those friends*.

The practice of welcoming people from another culture includes:

- Evaluating your own heart for any mistaken beliefs or prejudice
- Making the first move: introducing yourself and finding out their name and place of origin
- Showing an interest in them, their family, and their home culture
- Including them in family activities (meals, holiday celebrations, picnics, game nights, church events)
- Meeting practical needs or connecting them with someone who can
- Praying that God will open their minds and hearts to understand who Jesus is
- Looking for opportunities to share about Jesus and what He means to you

Welcoming unreached peoples who live in our communities changes their current reality. They meet believers who can share the gospel with them and demonstrate what it looks like to follow Jesus in everyday life, while helping them seek out answers to their questions. They may become among the first from their people group to receive Christ, and your friendship could become the catalyst for a movement of the Holy Spirit that could influence their unreached family, friends, and co-workers.

Welcoming unreached peoples also changes our families. We learn to interact with those who are different from us without fear or prejudice. We gain experience in demonstrating God's compassion to those who do not know Him as Savior. Our confidence in speaking to people from different religious backgrounds increases and we learn to share our own faith in a non-confrontational way.

If you are interested in learning more about welcoming, see *Xplore: Welcoming the Nations Among Us* in the Additional Resources section.

Habit: Go

Going, the most familiar of the five World Christian habits, is a straightforward response to Jesus' command to "go into all the world and preach the gospel to all creation" (Mark 16:15).

Re-read Luke 10:2.

[*What does Jesus say about the balance between the size of the global harvest and the number of workers in it?*]

> **Going**—ongoing practice of loving and serving among a people group whose culture is quite different from our own to reach them with the truth about Jesus; often involves moving or traveling to a distant area

In the harvest field are billions of unreached peoples who are waiting for someone to tell them about Jesus, but few are going to them. For example, there are about two or three Christian workers per 1 million Muslims.[8]

God is inviting families just like yours to go. What might this look like?

Some families will go long-term. They will live among the people group they minister to, investing time and effort in learning the local language and customs, cultivating friendships, demonstrating the love of Jesus, and sharing the gospel.

In places where families live in close proximity to unreached people groups, they may make frequent trips to minister to the unreached rather than living among them.

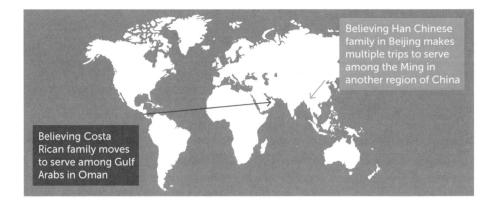

Believing Han Chinese family in Beijing makes multiple trips to serve among the Ming in another region of China

Believing Costa Rican family moves to serve among Gulf Arabs in Oman

A great starting place for families is to go and support the ongoing work of long-term workers or local churches serving among the unreached.

Going to serve among unreached peoples changes their current reality. They have an opportunity, perhaps their first, to hear and learn about Jesus. They have tangible models of what it looks like to follow Jesus in everyday life. Through discipleship and establishing local churches, those who become believers grow in their faith and learn how to share the good news of Jesus with others, multiplying the gospel in their community and region.

Going also changes our families. It gives us a bigger picture of who God is as we see Him reflected in different cultures. It increases our dependence on God as we are stretched out of our comfort zone and forced to navigate daily life without our familiar support structures. It grows our faith as we see God show up in miraculous ways in our own lives, and in the lives of the people we serve.

Think About It

[*Think about the habits of welcoming and going. How are they the same? How are they different?*]

_____

_____

_____

_____

[*Why do you think many believers are reluctant to consider "going" as an option for their own family?*]

_____

_____

_____

_____

Habit: Send

Another way that your family can bless unreached peoples is through the habit of sending.

Senders partner with cross-cultural goers who serve among people groups who have never heard or learned about Jesus.

> **Sending**—ongoing practice of using our resources to support cross-cultural goers who serve among the unreached; includes giving money, meeting their needs, encouraging them, and praying for their work

In Romans, Paul describes the process by which unreached peoples come to know and trust in Jesus. As senders, your family can play a strategic role in this process.

Read Romans 10:14-15. Look at the five key steps shown in the diagram. Underline the step that describes what senders do.

HOW UNREACHED PEOPLES COME TO FAITH

goers are sent to unreached > goers preach to the unreached > unreached hear the gospel > unreached believe in Jesus > unreached call on God to save them

[*If the sending step were removed, what would be the impact on cross-cultural goers? On the unreached?*]

_____

_____

_____

As senders, your family can support cross-cultural goers, enabling them to get to the field and stay on the field. Your ongoing, monthly financial support is crucial. Faithful giving by families like yours enables cross-cultural goers to focus on their ministry to the unreached rather than on how to provide for the daily needs of their own family.

Sending also includes practical actions like:

- Meeting goers' needs (give ride to the airport, arrange housing during home visits)
- Encouraging and appreciating goers (send birthday cards or favorite treats)
- Helping goers know they are not forgotten (send texts with news from home)
- Praying for goers' family and ministry needs (stay current through their newsletter or online chats)

Sending cross-cultural goers to unreached peoples changes their current reality. As more cross-cultural goers are sent out into God's harvest field through the sacrificial partnership of senders, more unreached people groups have the opportunity to hear and respond to the gospel.

Sending also changes our families. We recognize God as the source of blessing and realize that He blesses our family for a purpose that goes beyond ourselves. We become mindful of God's mission as we make choices about how we invest our time, talent, and treasure. Our family's compassion for the unreached grows as we invest in ministry to them.

Habit: Mobilize

Earlier, we learned that God invites us to join in His work. Families who practice mobilizing are excited about this invitation and want their friends to join them. They continually share God's mission and heart for the unreached with other believers they know.

Mobilizing happens in the context of your family's current relationships. It involves both *invitation* and *demonstration*...and results in *multiplication*.

Invitation:

Mobilizers are people whose lives have been transformed by the knowledge of God's purposes and who want to passionately share what they have learned with others. Think about friends and other families in your community. List 2-3 individuals/families whom you would love to tell about God's global heart and purposes:

_____

_____

_____

Demonstration:

An effective way to practice mobilizing in your family is to include other believing friends in your own ongoing practice of the World Christian habits.

> **Mobilizing**—ongoing practice of casting vision for God's global heart and purposes, raising awareness of the unreached, and equipping and inviting believers to join in God's work

As you model praying, sending, welcoming, or going, your friends see a firsthand demonstration of what joining God's work looks like in the everyday rhythms of family life. As they observe your involvement, you have the opportunity to invite them into practicing the World Christian habits as well.

What might demonstrating habits look like? Imagine this scenario ...

Your family fixes a meal that is commonly eaten by the Riffians, an unreached Muslim people group in North Africa. After dinner, you locate the region where this unreached people group lives on a world map. While your children place their hands on Northwest Africa, you intercede for the Riffians, asking God to send workers to tell them about Jesus.

[*In this scenario, what habit is your family practicing?*] _____

[*If another family joined you as you learned, ate, and prayed, what would they learn?*]

_____

_____

_____

_____

_____

Multiplication:

Mobilizers actively invite others into God's story and demonstrate ways they can be involved, resulting in more and more believers caring about the unreached peoples. Mobilization multiplies the number of people involved in God's story.

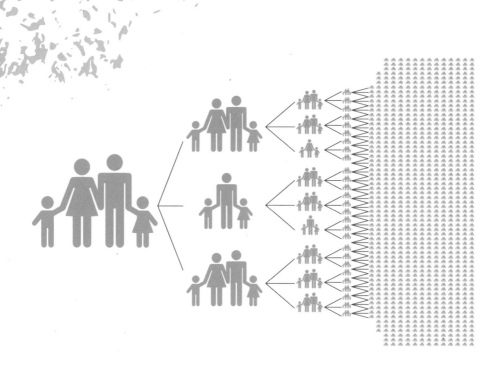

Mobilizing others towards unreached peoples changes their current reality. More believers become aware of God's plan for them and their situation. More believers join in praying, sending, and going to them, as well as welcoming the unreached who live in their own community. Efforts to bring the gospel to them are multiplied.

Mobilizing also changes our families. We have the joy of inviting our friends into God's work. Our own passion and commitment grow as we share about God's mission with others. We celebrate increased opportunities for unreached peoples to learn about Jesus as we partner with others in God's mission.

Pray, Welcome, Go, Send, Mobilize—just like forming any habit that becomes second nature, developing World Christian habits in your home will take intentionality, practice, consistency, and time. As parents, trust in God's Spirit to empower you each step of the way.

You may need to try different approaches to find out what works best for your family in this particular season of life. Readjust when needed and keep moving forward in the knowledge that God's work will be accomplished.

Think About It

[*How might incorporating the World Christian habits into your family's life shape your children's overall view of what being a follower of Jesus is all about?*]

_____

_____

_____

_____

_____

_____

_____

[*What excites you about participating in God's work as a family?*]

_____

_____

_____

_____

_____

_____

_____

God is inviting our families into the most exciting work on the planet—joining with Him in blessing all peoples with the good news of the gospel. Practicing the World Christian habits in our homes is the way we respond "yes" to God's invitation.

Live It Out

1. God blesses us to be a blessing to unreached people groups who do not know Him. Consider your time, talent, treasure, and where God has placed each family member during a typical week. With your spouse, or by yourself, list 5-10 ways that God has blessed your family. Spend time praying this week, asking God to show you how you might leverage these blessings as you begin to practice the World Christian habits in your family.

   _____

   _____

   _____

   _____

   _____

   _____

2. Practice being a mobilizer. Share something you learned about God's story and unreached peoples with a friend. Invite him or her to practice a World Christian habit with you.

3. Read One Big Adventure (part of the *Big Story Series* - *weavefamily.org/bigstoryseries*) to your children. Ask your children which of the five habits they would like to try. For ideas of ways to get started, read the section for parents on pages 33-38.

GROUP DISCUSSION GUIDE

Checking In (15 minutes)

Have someone in the group open in prayer. Before beginning the group discussion questions, briefly check in with one another about your initial reflections from the Lesson 4 personal study.

- What Bible verse or teaching point from Lesson 4 encouraged you or expanded your thinking?
- What activity from the Lesson 4 "Live It Out" section did you enjoy most?

Group Discussion (30 minutes)

Talk through each question, allowing all group members the opportunity to share their thoughts.

1. Many believers view going as a pursuit best undertaken by seminary students, pastors, evangelists, and others with a unique set of qualifications. What underlying assumptions support this belief? How might a paradigm shift that includes parents and their children as potential goers occur in your cultural context?

2. Suppose that your family desires to bless unreached peoples through sending. Discuss how you might find a cross-cultural goer who is serving, or preparing to serve, among the unreached. Where would you start and who could you ask for a recommendation?

3. Review the paragraph about World Christians on page 50. If living out the World Christian habits is rooted in the desire to see God glorified among all people groups, what practical steps could you take to cultivate this desire in your own family? How would living out the World Christian habits in your family serve to strengthen this desire even more?

OPTIONAL: Group Activity (10 minutes)

If your group has extra time or is meeting for longer than 60 minutes, complete this activity together. If not, move on to Group Prayer.

Have each person in the group finish this statement using one of the images below and explain their choice:

Integrating the World Christian habits into my family discipleship is like ___ because...

Group Prayer (10-15 minutes)

Close your time by praying for each other. Pray for God to:

- Show you how to incorporate the World Christian habits at home in ways that best fit your family's current season of life.
- Provide guidance in how to use your family's unique skills, passions, resources, and spiritual gifts as you live out the World Christian habits.

LESSON 5

Preparing Children to Launch

Personal Study

Like arrows in the hands of a warrior are

children born in one's youth. Blessed is

the man whose quiver is full of them.

—PSALM 127:4-5

Arrows and Archers

Think about arrows ...

In the hands of a skilled archer, arrows are extremely useful. However, arrows cannot function independently from the person who draws back the bowstring and releases them. They depend on the archer to determine both their purpose and path.

In the process of ongoing family discipleship, parents take on the role of the archer and the children in our homes become arrows. In Lesson 2, we learned that God entrusts fathers and mothers with the task of intentionally discipling our own children during the everyday moments of life to love God and His purposes.

As parents, we have the primary responsibility for preparing, aiming, and releasing our sons and daughters out into the world. The direction they take is greatly influenced by us.

Complete the idea in the box below by listing your children's names on the lines.

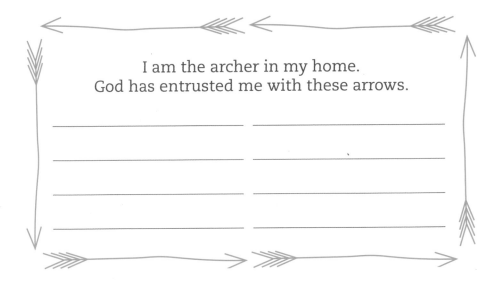

I am the archer in my home.
God has entrusted me with these arrows.

In this lesson, we will learn how God's mission connects to our purpose for launching our children out into the world. We will also explore the potential of children and why it is important to begin preparing and aiming them in the right direction now, while they are still young.

Targets

Before an archer shoots his arrows, he needs to have a clear target. The same is true in the process of discipling our children.

Without a well-defined target at which to aim, we run the risk of aiming at nothing, scattering our arrows so widely that they make little impact or allowing the culture in which we live to dictate our target for us.

Knowing the bigger purpose behind discipling our children creates intentionality in our home. Having an idea of the end goal helps us choose what to focus on as we disciple our children now.

Instead of becoming overwhelmed by situations and opportunities that flood into our lives on a daily basis, we begin to make strategic decisions and choices based on the direction we are moving in our family discipleship.

If today's discipleship decisions should be made with the end goal in mind, then as parents, we need to answer an important question:

Why are we launching our children out into the world?

The good news is that God does not expect parents to answer this question on our own. He already has a purpose in mind for our "arrows" and He is gracious enough to share this purpose with us! In fact, we have already learned many things about God's purposes in this study.

God has one main purpose, a mission He is pursuing throughout His story: to be known and worshiped among every people group. God's strategy for accomplishing His purpose began with a family and has included generations of Jesus-following families down through the ages.

Although God has been working through faithful families for thousands of years, His mission has yet to be achieved. Millions of people in our world are still waiting to hear about Jesus.

This is where your family comes in. Your ongoing participation in God's work helps to narrow the gap between today's current spiritual reality and God's end goal.

Review Lesson 4. List three ways that intentionally practicing the World Christian habits with your children can change the current spiritual reality of unreached peoples and bring God glory.

1. _____

2. _____

3. _____

As those from unreached people groups come into a relationship with Jesus, God receives the worship He deserves.

From what we have learned so far, we can see that God's purpose is clear and unchanging—He *will* be worshiped by some from every people group. God is aiming at a well-defined target—the realization of Revelation 7:9.

AFTER THIS I LOOKED, AND THERE BEFORE ME WAS A GREAT MULTITUDE THAT NO ONE COULD COUNT, FROM EVERY NATION, TRIBE, PEOPLE AND LANGUAGE, STANDING BEFORE THE THRONE AND BEFORE THE LAMB. THEY WERE WEARING WHITE ROBES AND WERE HOLDING PALM BRANCHES IN THEIR HANDS.

REVELATION 7:9

As the archers in our homes, we do not need to wonder about why we are launching our children out into the world. We can embrace God's purpose as our own.

We do not need to wonder about the direction in which we should aim our arrows. *God's* target becomes *our* target. We follow God's lead, aiming our children so they move in the same direction that He is moving.

If God has determined to make Himself known and worshiped among all people groups, and will not stop until this purpose is accomplished, then making God famous among all people groups should be a central focus of our family discipleship now, and a primary reason that we launch our children out into the world in the future.

Think About It

[*What would family discipleship look like in your home if you intentionally aimed your children at God's target?*]

_____

_____

_____

[*How does God's purpose for launching your children out into the world differ from what your culture tells you as parents?*]

_____

_____

_____

Quivers

Quivers serve as a temporary holding place for the archer's arrows, keeping them safe and secure until they are ready to be used.

However, arrows were not designed to remain in the quiver for a long period of time. Arrows fulfill their purpose only after they are removed from the quiver and released.

It is the same with the arrows God has entrusted to us. God created the children in our families to be used for His glory—not only when they are older, but now, when they are young. He invites our sons and daughters to join in His purpose to make Himself known and worshiped among all people groups.

As parents, however, we often desire to keep our children safe and secure, like arrows in a quiver. We are reluctant to launch them until they are much older.

Behind this delay is the belief that young children are not wise enough, mature enough, or experienced enough to participate in spiritual matters. Often, our beliefs about our children's capabilities are based on our culture's view rather than God's.

[*What do most adults in your culture believe that children are capable of and expected to do?*]

_____

_____

_____

[*What do most adults in your culture believe that children are incapable of doing until they grow up?*]

_____

_____

_____

God views the arrows in our quiver differently. To get insight into God's perspective, read Matthew 21:12-17. At the temple, Jesus encountered four groups of people.

Circle the group that God used to proclaim Jesus' identity as the Son of David to the people nearby.

merchants   blind and lame

chief priests/teachers of the law   children

If we were writing this part of God's story, we might have selected a religious scholar, or at least a mature adult, to reveal who Jesus was. Instead God used a group of excited children.

Rather than pushing these children aside or discounting their efforts, Jesus accepted them as they were and welcomed their worship. In fact, Jesus reminded the religious leaders that, "'From the lips of children and infants you, Lord, have called forth your praise" (Matthew 21:16, Psalm 8:2).

God doesn't just love and accept children. He also gives them active roles as characters in His story.

Read two true accounts of how God worked through children.

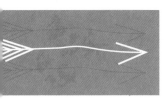

A young boy stood in the crowd that surrounded Jesus. He held a small basket containing his next meal—five small barley loaves and two bite-sized fish. As Jesus' disciples approached, taking stock of the amount of food available, they discovered him among the hungry crowd. Jesus used this boy's small gift of food to feed more than 5,000 men, women, and children. This young boy had a part in something big that happened on the hillside that day. Because of his willingness to share, and the power of Jesus to multiply, people in the crowd were amazed and recognized Jesus as the Prophet they were expecting (John 6).

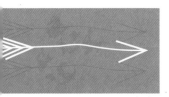

Eight-year-old Natalie donated all that she had earned to help translate the Bible into the language of an unreached Hindu people group. That money could have paid for ice cream, toys, or movie tickets. What motivated Natalie to help people she had never met who lived on the other side of the world? Here is a peek into Natalie's heart: "I started a club with some friends. We help neighbors in our community with chores. Most people pay us. We were going to use the money for something else, but when I heard that the Duga* people don't have Bibles, I decided to use the money to help them." God used Natalie's small gift, along with the gifts of many other believers, to communicate the truth of who He is to the Duga* people in their own heart language. *NAME CHANGED FOR SECURITY REASONS

Look at the phrases below. Check all the ideas that describe the children in these two accounts.

☐ OFFERED GOD WHAT THEY HAD

☐ UNIVERSITY GRADUATES

☐ QUICK TO RESPOND

☐ USED BY GOD

☐ YEARS OF EXPERIENCE IN PROBLEM SOLVING

☐ PRESENTED WITH AN OPPORTUNITY TO SERVE

☐ WELL-RESPECTED MEMBERS OF SOCIETY

☐ PARTICIPATED IN A PURPOSE BIGGER THAN THEMSELVES

☐ BIBLE SCHOLARS

☐ CHILDLIKE FAITH

☐ MATURE ADULTS

☐ BLESSED OTHERS

Neither of these children served out of his or her own strength. Instead, God's power worked through them. As the children offered what they had to Jesus, He multiplied their efforts and used them to bless many other people.

When you look at your own children, do you merely see the *smallness* of what they have to offer or do you have a *big* vision for God's work in and through their lives?

Just like the children in these two accounts, our own children can:

- embrace God's compassion for the peoples of the world and understand their needs.
- become involved in a purpose bigger than themselves.
- be a blessing to others when presented with age-appropriate opportunities.

Taking Aim

God wants us to remove the arrows from our quiver and aim them at the target long before we release them. This practice helps shape and strengthen our arrows and points them in the intended direction before they take flight.

Opportunities to serve God and experience Him for themselves will shape and strengthen our children's faith. Consistently aligning our children with the target of God's mission when they are young helps them know which direction to move as they launch out into adulthood.

In our family discipleship, we move beyond telling and modeling and intentionally involve our children in God's work. In Lesson 4, we learned that all believers, including parents *and their children*, can live out the World Christian habits.

On their own, young children may not be ready to *send* a cross-cultural worker to serve among the unreached or *welcome* people from other cultures. Your children can, however, practice these habits along with you in the context of family. Here are examples of child-sized opportunities to bless the nations.

Young Child

SEND: Put coins into a family jar with money designated for ministry to the unreached.

WELCOME: Make a welcome card for a refugee family from an unreached people group who has recently moved to your town.

Older Child

SEND: Have a monthly video chat with the children of cross-cultural workers.

WELCOME: Befriend a classmate from another country or culture and invite him to join in a family activity.

God sees the potential in our children. He invites them into His mission and empowers them to serve. As parents, we can foster an environment that enables our children to say "yes" to God's invitation in new ways at every age.

[*In what ways have your past interactions with your children encouraged or discouraged them from participating in God's work?*]

_____

_____

_____

_____

_____

Why Involve Children in God's Mission?

1. The task of making disciples among all nations is huge. It will take all of God's people to reach all of God's world.

Review Lesson 3 and fill in the blanks below.

_____ people groups have never heard of Jesus. This is _____ percent of the world's population.

"The harvest is plentiful, but the workers are few" (Luke 10:2). We need the entire body of Christ working together, including boys and girls who are learning to love and follow Jesus. Children are a strategic segment of God's church, and giving them opportunities to serve now helps them move from bystanders to participants.

2. Joining in God's mission gives our children a God-centered view of who they are and why they exist. As they participate in age-appropriate ways, our children develop an identity as active characters in God's eternal story!

I am a character in God's eternal story.

They understand that they were created to bring God glory. Realizing that they have a valuable role to play gives our children confidence and direction.

[*How does a God-centered view differ from the identity messages our children receive from mainstream culture?*]

_____

_____

3. By taking part in God's mission, our children gain a God-centered purpose. As children grow, they want to demonstrate that they can contribute in meaningful ways. We often see this desire reflected in the "Can I help?" question of young children and the tendency of older children to join causes that are important to them.

The desire for significance is also part of spiritual development. As children grow to love and obey Jesus, they want to serve Him in important ways and long to be committed to purposes that are bigger than themselves.

I'm a part of the greatest story of all.

When we offer our children opportunities to participate in God's mission, we aim them towards the most important purpose of all.

4. By consistently involving our children in God's mission while they are under our roof, we build lifelong habits in our sons and daughters that they will carry with them into adulthood.

Our adult children will become the next generation of parents. Our actions today will impact future generations of our family. Here are two examples of what this multigenerational impact might look like.

NOW   FUTURE

NOW	FUTURE
Consistently learn about God's mission and that God blesses them to be a blessing to the nations now.	Leverage their time, talents, and resources to align with God's mission ... and teach their own children to do the same.
Consistently learn about and practice the World Christian habits in child-friendly ways now.	Live out the World Christian habits in daily life ... and cultivate these habits in their own children.

Believing families who embrace and live out God's mission consistently, and who launch out adult sons and daughters who do the same things with their families, will be a significant part of seeing Revelation 7:9 realized.

Think About It

Read Proverbs 22:6.

[*How does this discipleship principle relate to consistently involving our children in God's mission while they are young?*]

_____

_____

_____

_____

_____

[*Imagine looking at a photo of your adult children 20 years from now. What do you want to be true of them? What is one step you can take in your family discipleship to help your children become the people that God created them to be?*]

_____

_____

_____

_____

What will we do with the arrows God has entrusted to us? Most Christian parents are satisfied with the kind of discipleship that leads their children into a relationship with Jesus and secures their future in heaven. Although this kind of discipleship is crucial to our children's eternal future, let's not stop there. Our children were not only saved *from* something ... they were saved *for* something.

Live It Out

1. During your devotions this week, read and meditate on one or more of the following accounts where God used children in His story: Miriam (Exodus 2:1-9), Samuel (1 Samuel 3:1-18), and Josiah (2 Kings 22:1-2, 23:25).

2. Choose one of the World Christian habits. Together with your spouse, or on your own, brainstorm several age-appropriate ways you could begin to engage your own children in this habit.

_____

_____

_____

3. If you haven't yet, download the *Big Story Series* for free from *weavefamily.org/bigstoryseries*. From One Big Story, do the "A Commander's Heart Changed" family devotion found on page 20 with your children. Talk with them about how God can use children like them in His story.

GROUP DISCUSSION GUIDE

Checking In (15 minutes)

Have someone in the group open in prayer. Before beginning the group discussion questions, briefly check in with one another about your initial reflections from the Lesson 5 personal study.

- What Bible verse or teaching point from Lesson 5 encouraged you or expanded your thinking?
- What activity from the Lesson 5 "Live It Out" section did you enjoy most?

Group Discussion (30 minutes)

Talk through each question, allowing all group members the opportunity to share their thoughts.

1. Consider the "arrows" in your own "quiver." When you think about releasing your children into God's mission, what makes you hesitant? What insights from this lesson encouraged you in this area?

2. Serving God and putting His mission first may result in our lifestyles looking far different from those around us. How do we teach our children that the purpose of their lives is to be faithful to God and His mission, not to achieve success in the way the world defines it?

3. As we help our children develop their skills, talents, and interests, how do we set aside personal and cultural expectations, replacing them with a motive of service to God and His global purposes?

OPTIONAL: Group Activity (10 minutes)

If your group has extra time or is meeting for longer than 60 minutes, complete this activity together. If not, move on to Group Prayer.

Read the statement below. Have each person share his/her response to the statement and then write it in the target:

Considering all I have learned in this study, here are two things I need to add to the target at which I'm aiming my "arrows."

Group Prayer (10-15 minutes)

Close your time by praying for each other. Pray for God to:

- Open your eyes and heart to the potential of your children to play an active role in God's story.
- Give you opportunities to bless and reach the nations as a family at every stage of your children's development.

LESSON 6

Pressing Forward

Personal Study

Never concede to doing something so small that it could be accomplished entirely in your lifetime. Be a part of something that began before you were born, and will continue onward toward the fulfillment of all that God has purposed to accomplish.

—RALPH WINTER

Setting a New Course

Congratulations! You have persevered and made it to the last lesson in this study. When it comes to implementing family discipleship in your home, however, you may feel like you are standing on the starting line.

Before beginning Lesson 1, you gave responses to six ideas, based on your personal knowledge at that time. Take some time to reflect on what you have learned in this study and how it has shifted or expanded your perspective.

Review your answers from the Pre-Study Reflection. Then, in the left column under "Before the Study," write a short summary of your perspective prior to the study. In the right column, record changes in your perspective.

Before the Study	After the Study

How I view my responsibility to disciple my children

How I view and teach the Bible

How I view my family's blessings

How I view what discipling my children looks like

Before the Study | After the Study

How I view the peoples of the world

How I view God's purposes for my family

How I view the role families can play in God's mission

How I view the potential of my children to engage in God's work

As parents we are in a continuous learning process, both in our own faith walk with God and in the way we disciple our children. Satan would love to discourage us by pointing out areas in which we have failed with our children or convince us that it is too late to change the way we are discipling them.

However, the Christian life is one of second chances, new beginnings, and ongoing transformation. As God's Spirit reveals new things to us as parents, we need to respond in obedience. Often this response involves revising current patterns and, with God's help, beginning to move in a new direction.

Read Ephesians 3:20-21 and 2 Peter 1:3.

[*How do these verses encourage you as you consider how to incorporate concepts from this study in your family discipleship?*]

It is helpful to remember that although God chooses us to be the primary disciplers of our children, He does not expect us to lead them on our own. He is the one who empowers and equips us with everything we need.

Beginning to disciple our children in God's mission is likely to require making adjustments to the way we have led them in the past, developing new practices and rhythms in our homes. This process will require both patience and perseverance on our part because it takes time for new habits to become fully established.

The good news is that discipling our children to love God and embrace His purposes is more like a long-distance marathon than a short sprint. It is all right to begin slowly and create a strong foundation on which we can continue to build our family discipleship for years to come.

Basic Equipment

All runners need the same basic gear when they begin training. As they grow as runners, they will add routines and equipment which are tailored to suit their needs.

As we incorporate family discipleship in our homes, we need to start with the fundamentals. Three components that are foundational to our ongoing family discipleship are:

God's Word   God's world   God's work

God's Word:

The Bible is our primary resource for discipling our children. In our world of constant change, "the word of our God endures forever" (Isaiah 40:8). In our world of multiple, competing opinions, "the word of the Lord is right and true" (Psalm 33:4). Amid claims that there are many paths to God, God's Word lays out a singular, clear pathway through Jesus, "the way and the truth and the life" (John 14:6).

Our children need to know God's story and what He asks of us through His Word. Gathering as a family and studying the Bible together on a weekly basis is the best way to do so. We also want to teach our children how to do personal devotions as they get older.

The more informal discipleship we learned about in Lesson 2 can support more formal learning that takes place during family Bible study. We can use everyday moments and familiar objects throughout the week to reinforce concepts and answer questions that arise from our family Bible study.

Many families find it helpful to set aside a specific time each week to prioritize reading and discussing God's Word together. You will need to prioritize this time like you would any other ongoing commitment.

Look at your weekly schedule and the current commitments of all family members. Choose a day or evening when everyone is usually home and when your children are most alert. Write down a day and time when you could incorporate 15-20 minutes of unrushed, concentrated family Bible time.

Day: _____   Time: _____

In family Bible study, the aim is to help our children see their lives as a part of God's eternal story rather than isolated from it. We want them to view themselves in light of God's global heart and mission and to understand the greater purpose behind God's blessings in their lives.

This requires us to adjust how we share God's Word with our children. We do not alter the Bible text, but rather change the way we talk about and apply Bible passages with our children.

Through our words, we strive to consistently emphasize these concepts:
- The Bible is God's story and He is the main character.
- God's mission is to make Himself known and worshiped among every people group.
- God is always working towards the fulfillment of His mission.
- God blesses His followers so that they will be a blessing to all peoples of the earth.

Let's explore what it might look like to integrate these concepts into our family Bible study. Imagine that your family has just read the story of Daniel in the lion's den together (Daniel 6).

Here are four ways of discussing the Daniel 6 passage. Circle two that focus on *both* God's blessing and the greater purpose behind it.

How did God protect Daniel from the lions?	How did God bless Daniel in the lion's den? What other people heard about the true God?
How did God intervene in Daniel's situation? How did God use Daniel's experience to change the king's heart?	How did God rescue Daniel in the lion's den?

Imagine if you consistently discussed Bible stories in ways similar to those you circled. How would it expand your children's view of what God is doing in our world and how He wants to work through His people?

_____

_____

_____

Here are two valid ways of applying the Daniel 6 passage to our lives. Circle the application that includes a component which helps children see how God can use them in His story to bless others.

During the week, when might we need to stand strong for our faith? God is always with us, just like He was with Daniel. We can pray and ask God for help and courage in these situations.	During the week, when might we need to stand strong for our faith? An unbelieving king observed Daniel. Who are the unbelievers who might be watching us? What might they learn about God by observing how we stand up for our faith? We can pray and ask God for help and courage in these situations.

Consistently sharing the Bible in these ways will have a huge impact on our children. They will begin to view historical and current events, as well as situations in their own lives, through the lens of God's eternal purposes. They will also gain a balanced perspective on why God blesses them.

God's world:

If God invites our families to join with Him in blessing all nations with the gospel of Jesus, then our children need to understand who the unreached people groups are, where they live, what their lives are like, and what they believe. In our homes, we need to be always learning about unreached peoples and praying that they would have the opportunity to hear about Jesus.

Choose a different unreached people group to focus on every month. Learn something about their culture each week. Make your learning time fun and memorable by including hands-on activities that your family can participate in together. The ideas are endless!

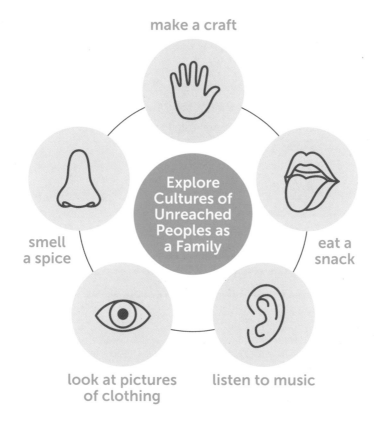

make a craft

smell a spice

Explore Cultures of Unreached Peoples as a Family

eat a snack

look at pictures of clothing

listen to music

Keep a world map handy and use it to locate where the unreached people group you are learning about lives. Learn about their religious beliefs and how these beliefs compare to God's Word. Pray for this people group throughout the month.

God's work:

To build a lifetime habit of joining God in His mission, we need to live out the five World Christian habits with our children throughout the year. Make them a regular part of who your family is and what you do together.

Here are some ideas you can incorporate in your home:

- Build intercessory prayer habits into your learning about God's world (pray).
- Invest financially in mission work among the unreached and look for ways to emotionally support those serving among them (send).
- Build intentional relationships with people from different cultures in your community (welcome).
- Invite other families to join you in learning about God's mission and the unreached; practice the World Christian habits together (mobilize).
- Be open to God calling your family to minister among the unreached (go).

As your children grow up, try different ideas that match their age and developmental level. The key is to be intentional and stay consistent. When we create opportunities to involve our children in God's work at every stage of life, they will view joining in God's mission as central to their walk with Jesus.

First Steps

As parents, not all of us are at the same point in the marathon process of discipling our children. Maybe you are feeling overwhelmed and are not sure where to start. Every race begins with a first step. Begin with one of the fundamentals we talked about in the previous section—God's Word, God's world, or God's work. Then build on that foundation. It's not about how fast you start; it's about sustaining a consistent pace over a long period of time.

In summary, here are three steps for incorporating God's Word, God's world, and God's work into your family discipleship, along with how the *Big Story Series* resources (introduced earlier in this study) can help. If you haven't already, you can download this resource free at *weavefamily.org/bigstoryseries*.

1. *God's Word:* Study the Bible together as a family each week. Discuss specific passages in the context of God's primary mission. Apply stories to your family's life using the "blessed to be a blessing" pattern. For examples of how to introduce, discuss, and apply Bible stories in these ways, refer to *One Big Story*.

2. *God's world:* Learn about and pray for unreached people groups. Start by focusing on an unreached people group in your own city or country. Introduce new groups gradually until you establish a rhythm of learning about and praying for a different unreached people group every month. Refer to *One Big Vision* for child-friendly information on unreached people groups and ideas for how to teach about non-Christian worldviews.

3. *God's work:* Choose one or two World Christian habits that best fit your family's season of life. Live out these habits with your children throughout the year. To review the habits, or find specific ideas for living them out, refer to *One Big Adventure.*

If you are just beginning to disciple your children in God's mission, choose an idea from one of the three foundational areas to try with your family. Be consistent in implementing it in your home. Once you have established a rhythm that feels natural, add another idea.

The *Big Story Series* can help you develop your own knowledge and skills in these three areas and help you take small, consistent steps in creating a discipleship plan that works for your family.

Maybe you are already part of the way down the track in your family discipleship but feel the need to adjust your approach, or add something new, to better align with God's global heart and purposes. Do not get discouraged or drop out of the race. Rely on the fundamentals to help you revise your current course.

Continue to go deeper in each of the three foundational areas as your children grow older. Choose ideas from the *Big Story Series* to support or supplement resources you already use. Be sensitive to specific ways that God is inviting your family to become a blessing to the nations.

Here are two examples of how families have incorporated God's Word, world, and work into their discipleship.

Wu Family, China:

After going through this parent study, both Mom and Dad realized the importance of taking a much bigger role in discipling their two children. They started with what they knew best— God's Word. After looking at their busy schedule, they chose Friday evenings to begin having family devotions. Each week, they did one Bible lesson from One Big Story. *A few months later, Mom and Dad added learning about unreached people groups into their family devotional time. As the family began to do activities from* One Big Vision, *both parents realized that God was preparing their children's hearts, giving them a desire to intercede for the unreached! Each night before dinner, the Wus prayed for the people group they were learning about that month.*

While using One Big Vision, *the family read a story about the Kham Tibetans. Mom knew that a family from that people group lived right in their own apartment complex. The Wus introduced themselves to this family and began to build a relationship with them. Based on what God was laying on their hearts, and the opportunities He placed before them, the Wu family incorporated the World Christian habits of praying and welcoming into their annual rhythm. The Wus are so excited about what God has been teaching them that they have invited another family from their house church to join them for devotions. Now that family has begun weekly devotions in their own home!*

Navarro Family, Mexico:

On Sunday evenings, Mr. and Mrs. Navarro do a family devotion with their three children before enjoying a meal together. After completing this parent study, both parents realized that although they had been teaching their children about who God is and His love for them, they had never talked about God's purposes for those blessings. Dad started reframing family devotions to talk about how God had blessed their family so they could be a blessing to the others.

Mom printed out the unreached people group coloring pages from One Big Vision. *Every month, their family reads about one of the people groups in that resource while their children color the matching picture. Each child hangs their coloring page by their bed as a reminder to pray for that people group each night during the month. The Navarros also researched an organization in their country that sends cross-cultural workers to take the gospel to unreached Muslim people groups in Asia. Their family committed to financially supporting one of these workers each month.*

Moving Forward Together

Most marathon racers experience increased performance when they run together in a group. Because runners pace each other, they tend to go faster than they would alone. Mutual encouragement and accountability help runners persevere and go farther.

Read Proverbs 27:17, Ecclesiastes 4:9-10, and Hebrews 10:24-25.

[*According to these verses, what are the benefits of living out our faith with, and alongside, other believers?*]

_____

_____

_____

_____

Discipling your children alongside a group of like-minded parents will help you develop fresh ideas and persevere when you feel like giving up. If you have already been doing this study with other parents, consider continuing to meet together. Discuss how you are implementing aspects of God's Word, world, and work in your discipleship. Share ideas that are working well, problem-solve together, and pray for one another. See Appendix III for more ideas.

If you went through this parent study by yourself, think bigger. It is awesome that your family is responding to God's invitation to join with Him in blessing the nations with the good news of Jesus. As we learned in Lesson 5, however, the Great Commission task is huge. Many more believing families are needed to reach all of God's world.

Imagine what might happen if you weren't the only parents who were discipling your family to step into God's story. Think about how you might mobilize other families to do likewise.

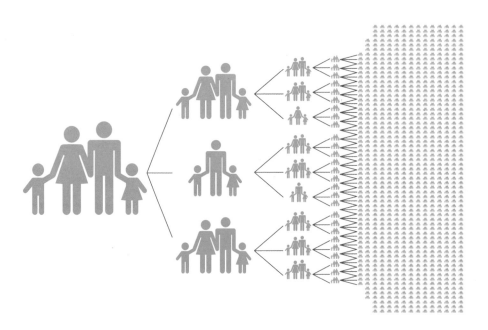

Whether you went through this parent study by yourself or with others, you can use these materials to take more parents through this same study with you.

The lessons are designed so that any parent who has gone through them, and is beginning to implement some of the suggestions in their home, can easily lead others through the same process.

Think about groups of parents that already meet together on a regular basis with whom you could do this study—a community group at church, parents group at school, Christian moms or dads that you connect with informally—or create your own group.

Find a time when you could meet together. Elicit help from others in the group to organize the meetings. Use the Group Discussion Guide at the end of each lesson to guide your conversations.

Think About It

[*List two ways that you would personally benefit from discipling your children in community.*]

_____

_____

_____

_____

_____

[*Make a list of existing groups, or individual parents you know, who would benefit from going through this parent study along with you.*]

_____

_____

_____

_____

_____

Discipling our children to love God and to live out His purposes throughout their lives is a long-term commitment. Sometimes the process is difficult and demanding, but it can also be joyful and rewarding.

Be encouraged that God's Holy Spirit is with you every step of the way, and move forward in the confidence "that He who began a good work in you will carry it on to completion until the day of Christ Jesus" (Philippians 1:6).

Live It Out

1. Every long-distance race starts with a first step. With your spouse, or by yourself, assess where you are in your family discipleship right now. Identify the next 1-2 steps you will take as parents.

_____

_____

_____

_____

_____

_____

_____

_____

2. Think of a set of parents you know who are discipling their children at home on a regular basis. Invite them to join you for tea or coffee. Ask how they fit family discipleship into their weekly schedule and learn from them.

3. Think of other Christian parents who would benefit from what you have been learning in this study. Begin sharing with them about what God has been teaching you until you find one or two individuals or couples who would commit to going through this study with you.

Living Your Legacy

Discovering your family's vision statement

weave

Parents, do you have a story of how this study has impacted your own family discipleship?

Share it with us at weavefamily.org/pgv-impact and receive a free downloadable resource on creating your own family vision statement.

GROUP DISCUSSION GUIDE

Checking In (15 minutes)

Have someone in the group open in prayer. Before beginning the group discussion questions, briefly check in with one another about your initial reflections from the Lesson 6 personal study.

- What Bible verse or teaching point from Lesson 6 encouraged you or expanded your thinking?
- What activity from the Lesson 6 "Live It Out" section did you enjoy most?

Group Discussion (30 minutes)

Talk through each question, allowing all group members the opportunity to share their thoughts.

1. Think about the foundational components for discipling your family in God's mission—God's Word, God's world, and God's work. Which will be easiest for you to incorporate in your home? What will be most challenging and what is likely to distract you from following through?

2. Share about a habit that required effort for you to develop, but later became a natural part of your life. What elements are important in the process of building new habits? How do these elements apply to establishing new rhythms in your family discipleship?

3. Discuss some practical steps you can take to encourage one another and hold each other accountable as your families continue to grow in the areas of God's Word, God's world, and God's work. How might you widen your circle to include other families who could benefit from the ideas in this study?

OPTIONAL: Group Activity (10 minutes)

If your group has extra time or is meeting for longer than 60 minutes, complete this activity together. If not, move on to Group Prayer.

Have each person draw a quick sketch in the box to illustrate his/her response to the statement found there. Take turns sharing your reasoning with the group.

In the marathon of discipling my children in God's mission, I am currently at this point:

Group Prayer (10-15 minutes)

Close your time by praying for each other. Pray for God to:
- Give you creativity and wisdom in integrating God's Word, world, and work into your family discipleship.
- Provide you with opportunities to share the vision of discipling families in God's mission with other parents.

Appendices &
Additional Resources

Appendix I

31 Verses To Pray for Unreached Peoples

Read these Bible verses with unreached peoples in mind. Then turn the content of the verses into intercessory prayers for the unreached.

1. Psalm 22:27
2. Psalm 67:3
3. Psalm 86:9
4. Psalm 96:1-3
5. Psalm 96:7-8
6. Psalm 97:6
7. Isaiah 9:2
8. Isaiah 45:22
9. Isaiah 61:11
10. Ezekiel 36:26
11. Mark 16:15
12. Luke 10:2
13. John 3:16-17
14. John 14:6
15. Acts 2:38-39
16. Acts 4:12
17. Acts 11:20-21
18. Acts 26:18
19. Romans 1:16
20. Romans 6:23
21. Romans 10:13-15
22. 2 Corinthians 4:4
23. 2 Corinthians 5:17
24. Galatians 3:26
25. Ephesians 2:8-9
26. Philippians 2:9-11
27. Colossians 1:13-14
28. 1 Peter 2:10
29. 1 John 2:2
30. 1 John 4:9
31. Revelation 15:4

Appendix II

12 Everyday Objects and Moments

Use these familiar objects and moments in family life to teach your children more about God and His mission. Continue to use this pattern as you add your own ideas.

Object/Moment	God's Character	God's Mission
bread	God tells us to taste and see that He is good. We can not know if bread is good unless we taste it. We cannot experience the goodness of God unless we spend time with Him (Psalm 34:8).	Jesus is the bread of life that comes down from heaven. Jesus came to earth to die for our sins so He could offer eternal life to all the peoples in the world (John 6:32-35, 40).
bedtime	The Bible tells us that we can rest peacefully at night, knowing that God will make us dwell in safety (Psalm 4:8).	As we tell other people about Jesus, it is God who changes their hearts. We can rest in God's promise that He will be exalted among the nations (Psalm 46:10).
rock	The Bible tells us that God is our rock and our salvation. When He is our foundation, we will not be shaken (Psalm 62:6).	David used only a stone and a sling to defeat a giant. Through this unlikely victory, God demonstrated to the whole world that there was a God in Israel. Today, God still uses believers like us to show the peoples of the world who He is (1 Samuel 17:45-47).
family	The Bible says God loves us so much that when we put our trust in Jesus, we join His family. We become His children and He becomes our Heavenly Father (Galatians 3:26, 1 John 3:1-2).	The Bible tells us that one day all of the families of the nations will bow down before the Lord (Psalm 22:27).
candle/ light bulb	God's Word is like a light shining on a dark path. It helps us know how to follow Jesus (Psalm 119:105).	Jesus says that as believers, we can be like lights. Through our actions and words, we can point unbelievers to God (Matthew 5:14-16).
water	Jesus says that when we believe in Him, our hearts will flow with rivers of living water. This living water is His Spirit that dwells inside us (John 7:38-39).	The Bible tells us that one day the knowledge of the glory of God will fill the whole earth in the same way that the waters cover the whole sea (Habakkuk 2:14).

Object/Moment	God's Character	God's Mission
musical instrument/ singing	Playing music and singing helps us make a joyful noise to the Lord. God wants us to worship Him with joy and gladness (Psalm 100:1-2).	Heaven will celebrate the completion of God's plan to bring believers from every nation to heaven with a new song (Revelation 5:9).
tree/vine	Jesus is the vine, and we are the branches. A branch that is connected to a fig tree will produce a specific fruit—figs. When we stay connected to Jesus, we will speak and act more and more like Jesus (John 15:5).	In heaven, there will be a tree of life. God's purpose is to bring peoples from all nations into a relationship with Him and give them eternal life in His presence (Revelation 22:2-3).
wind	During a storm at sea, Jesus calmed the strong wind by speaking to it and telling it to stop. As God's Son, Jesus created all things in nature and has control over them (Matthew 8:23-27, Colossians 1:15-16).	The Bible says the Holy Spirit came on the disciples like a mighty wind from heaven, and they began to share the gospel in other languages. God desires all people to hear the gospel in a way they can understand (Acts 2:1-4).
door/gate	Jesus says He is the door, the only entrance into God's presence. Jesus died for our sins so we could come to God in faith (John 10:9).	God desires for all peoples to know Him. God opens doors of opportunity for believers to share their faith with those who have not yet heard (Colossians 4:3).
going to church	God created us for community. We can gather together as believers to learn from God's Word and pray together. A church is not just a building, but also followers of Jesus who meet together (Acts 2:42).	Jesus said He will build His church, but many people around the world have never heard about Him. We can pray for the gospel to spread to these people and for new communities of believers to be formed (Matthew 16:18).
feet/walking	God has created each of us in a special way and He has prepared good works for each believer to do that we can walk in. God designs us for the work He has in mind (Ephesians 2:10).	Our feet help us go. More and more people will hear about Jesus as we go and tell them. We need to go (Matthew 28:18-20)!

Appendix III

Community Activities

If you went through this study with a small group of parents, here are suggested activities you can do together to support one another in your next steps. Some activities will help you incorporate ideas from this study into your family discipleship. Others will help you mobilize more families to participate in God's story along with you.

1. Break into pairs. Take turns explaining what God's mission is. Repeat, but this time imagine that your partner is one of your own children.

2. Do a role-play activity in which some people are parents and others are children. Practice leading a family Bible time about David and Goliath (1 Samuel 17) for your children. Make sure to include both God's blessing and purpose.

3. Break into pairs. Choose an object from the "12 Everyday Objects and Moments" chart (Appendix II). Pretend your partner is six years old. Take turns using your object to teach them something about God's character or mission. Next, pretend that your partner is 12 years old. Take turns teaching them the same concept.

4. In pairs or small groups, do a role-play activity in which you share about the current spiritual state of the world with a Christian parent who has not done this study. Use information and hand motions from the Spiritual State of the World diagram in Lesson 3. Include the concept of unreached peoples in your explanation.

5. Get together with other families to learn and memorize some of Jesus' Great Commission passages: Matthew 28:19-20, Mark 16:15, Luke 24:46-47, John 20:21, and Acts 1:8. Add hand motions or music to help your children remember the verses.

6. Choose a few verses from "31 Verses to Pray for Unreached Peoples" (Appendix I) to read aloud. In pairs or small groups, practice turning these verses into prayers for the unreached.

7. Choose a specific unreached people group. With parents from the study and their children, eat a simple meal or snack which is common in the culture of this unreached people group. On a world map, locate where this group lives. Afterwards, spend time praying for them. Repeat this kind of activity a month later. This time, invite several families who did not go through the study to join you. Model how to learn about and pray for the unreached.

8. In pairs or small groups, do a role-play activity. Practice beginning a conversation with someone from another culture who lives in your community. Afterwards, go to an international market or restaurant as a group. Try out what you practiced.

9. Learn more about the religious beliefs of a people group in your area. Visit one of their places of worship with another family (examples: mosque; Hindu, Buddhist, or Daoist temple). Afterwards, discuss with the children how this group's beliefs contrast with the truth of the Bible. Pray together for God to open their eyes to the truth.

10. Work together with other parents from this study to find a "goer" who is serving, or preparing to serve, among the unreached. As a group of families, financially support this "goer" in an ongoing way.

Additional Resources

Receive ongoing ideas for discipling your family in God's Word, God's world, and God's work.

Weave newsletter: Emails include practical ways to help your family study God's Word with His bigger purposes in mind, learn about and pray for unreached peoples, and live out the World Christian habits in your home. Subscribe to receive two emails each month.

weavefamily.org

Grow in your own understanding of God's global heart and mission, unreached peoples, and the World Christian habits.

COURSES

Kairos:

9-session interactive course, available in several formats.

simplymobilizing.com/kairos

Perspectives on the World Christian Movement:

15-session interactive course, available in several formats.

perspectives.org

SMALL GROUP/HOME STUDIES

Xplore, Center for Mission Mobilization.

7-lesson study on God's Word, world, and work. Free download in multiple languages.

mobilization.org/xplore

Xplore: Welcoming the Nations Among Us, Center for Mission Mobilization.

6-lesson study on the World Christian habit of welcoming. Free download.

mobilization.org/welcoming

Go Mobilize, Center for Mission Mobilization.

7-lesson study on the World Christian habit of mobilizing. Follow-up to *Xplore.* Free download in multiple languages.

mobilization.org/gomobilize

Learn about the spiritual state of the world, five major non-Christian worldviews, and specific unreached people groups.

WEBSITES

joshuaproject.net

operationworld.org

peoplegroups.org/ReligionList.aspx

weavefamily.org/connect (child-friendly people group information)

VIDEOS

joshuaproject.net/pray/videos

prayercast.com/world-religions.html

youtube.com/c/WeaveFamily (videos created for children)

Endnotes

Lesson 3

1. Statistic from Joshua Project, *joshuaproject.net*
2. Statistic from Joshua Project, *joshuaproject.net*
3. Statistic from Joshua Project, *joshuaproject.net*
4. Statistic from Joshua Project, *joshuaproject.net*
5. Statistic from Joshua Project, *joshuaproject.net*
6. Statistic from "The Task Remaining" by Ralph D. Winter and Bruce Koch, *Perspectives on the World Christian Movement*, Reader. 4th ed. William Carey Library, 2009, p. 541.
7. Statistic from The Traveling Team, *thetravelingteam.org*

Lesson 4

8. Extrapolated from a statistic which states there is 1 missionary for every 405,500 Muslims. The Traveling Team, *thetravelingteam.org*

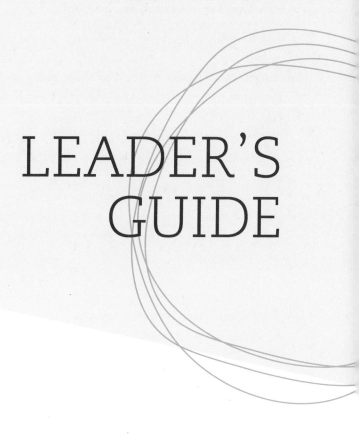

LEADER'S GUIDE

We are excited that you have decided to lead

a new group of parents through this study!

—THE WEAVE TEAM

God has given you the ability to lead.

As a disciple of the Savior of the world, you have been empowered to disciple others, helping them join with God in blessing the nations with the good news of Jesus.

We prayed for you long before this study was published. We asked God to raise up leaders who would guide other parents through this study, and His answer to that prayer is you!

Here is a step-by-step plan that will help you prepare and lead your study. If you need assistance at any step in the process, we are here to help. Please email us at info@weavefamily.org

1. Invite parents/friends to join you for this 6-week study. The Helpful Hints section provides helpful phrases to use. Parents with children between the ages of 4-12 will benefit most from this study. Invite both spouses if possible.

2. Calendar your study and set your first meeting time. If you'd like to gather parents for a separate introductory meeting, see tips in the Helpful Hints section.

3. Register your group here: weavefamily.org/pgv-registration

4. Inform parents they need to complete the Pre-study Reflection and Lesson 1 Personal Study before your first regular meeting. Make sure that parents understand that this will take between 1-2 hours.

5. Gather together for 60-75 minutes and use the Group Discussion Guide at the end of each lesson to guide your conversations.

6. Repeat the process for each lesson: each person completes the Personal Study on their own and then you come together for discussion using the Group Discussion Guide. For tips on facilitating a group, see the Helpful Hints section.

To know if parents in your group are grasping the primary concepts of each lesson, see Parent Study Key Ideas in the Helpful Hints section.

After your study concludes, consider going deeper with your group in understanding what family mobilization looks like and applying what you have learned in your own families. See a few ideas below.

Practice in Community

You've finished the study — wonderful! We pray that it was a transforming experience for each parent in your group. Learning together does not have to end here. Consider ways that you, as the group leader, can help guide your group to apply what was learned together. Discuss as a group continuing to meet together on a monthly basis for deeper learning, mutual support, encouragement, and accountability.

In your meeting times, use ideas from Appendix III and the Additional Resources sections of the book to help parents gain experience and confidence in discipling their children in God's mission. Encourage everyone in your group to download the *Big Story Series* to help them integrate God's Word, world, and work into their ongoing family discipleship.

Equip New Leaders

The task of reaching the remaining unreached peoples in the world requires more of God's people participating in His mission. Each person in your group knows other parents who they can mobilize. Think back on what prompted you to lead this study. You desired to share what you learned with friends. You wanted them to catch the vision of discipling their family in God's mission, just like you did. This study is designed so that any parent who has gone through it and is applying what they learned can easily lead others through the same process.

It is highly likely that leaders for future parent studies already exist within your current group. Here are ways you can identify and equip these potential leaders.

1. Follow up with those in your group, either in conversations as you continue to meet together or by sending them a message. See how parents are doing and inquire how they have used what they learned from the study. Take note of parents who are understanding and consistently applying key concepts from the study with their family. Also look for parents who are already sharing what they have learned with other parents they know.

2. Identify a parent/couple who has begun to consistently disciple their family. Invite them to co-lead a future parent study group with you to help them gain more experience before they lead on their own.

3. After co-leading a group together, encourage them to lead their own parent study group.

Helpful Hints

PREPARING YOURSELF TO LEAD:

Read through the Introduction section in the book to get a better understanding of how lessons are structured and what each section is designed to accomplish. Pray for God to move in the hearts and minds of each parent in your group, and for God to do mighty things in each family represented.

INVITATION TALKING POINTS:

Here are some helpful phrases you can include in your conversations or electronic invitations:

- Discover your family's role in God's story
- Become more intentional in leading your children spiritually
- Understand more of God's global heart and purposes
- Receive practical ways to be involved in God's work as a family

OPTIONAL SEVENTH WEEK:

Hold an introductory gathering before you begin the study where you:

- Get to know your group and learn more about each other's families.
- Give out the books or show parents how to download a digital copy.
- Explain the lesson format, weekly time commitment, and which sections parents need to complete before your first group discussion.
- Point out information on downloading the *Big Story Series* resources in the Introduction section of their book. Explain that several activities from these books are included in "Live it Out" sections of the study.

- You committed to lead this study, not to teach it. Relax, go on the journey with your group, and allow God to speak to each parent's heart in His own way.
- Don't be afraid of awkward silence. Be patient and allow time for your group to process their thoughts.
- Give everyone the opportunity to share. This may mean limiting some parents to shorter answers and gently drawing out others.

PARENT STUDY KEY IDEAS:

- Throughout His story, God is pursuing His mission to redeem and draw some from every people group to Him in worship.
- God blesses His people for the greater purpose of blessing the nations.
- God designs and equips parents to be the primary disciplers of their children.
- God invites families into His ongoing work of blessing the nations with the gospel.
- Children have the potential to participate in God's work from an early age.
- Unreached peoples have no access to the gospel. Few cross-cultural workers are going to them.
- Families can bless the unreached by practicing the World Christian habits in an ongoing way.
- God will accomplish His mission. He will be worshiped by some from every people group.

We'd love to hear how your study went and how parents are applying what they learned.

Email your stories to info@weavefamily.org.